THE GREAT
DIAMOND
HEIST

THE GREAT DIAMOND HEIST

THE TRUE STORY OF THE HATTON GARDEN ROBBERY

GORDON BOWERS

JOHN BLAKE

Published by John Blake Publishing Limited,
3 Bramber Court, 2 Bramber Road,
London W14 9PB, England

www.johnblakepublishing.co.uk

www.facebook.com/johnblakebooks ⬛
twitter.com/jblakebooks ⬛

First published in paperback in 2016

ISBN: 978-1-78418-978-5

British Library Cataloguing-in-Publication Data:
A catalogue record for this book is available from the British Library.

Design by www.envydesign.co.uk

Printed in Great Britain by CPI Group (UK) Ltd

1 3 5 7 9 10 8 6 4 2

Papers used by John Blake Publishing are natural, recyclable products made from
wood grown in sustainable forests. The manufacturing processes conform to the
environmental regulations of the country of origin.

Every attempt has been made to contact the relevant copyright-holders,
but some were unobtainable. We would be grateful if the appropriate people
could contact us.

CONTENTS

CHAPTER ONE

DOWN THE GARDEN PATH

I walked past the Hatton Garden Safe Deposit Company on that Easter Sunday just a few hours after the diamond heist gang had scarpered with their loot. I was on my way to have lunch with my elderly mother, who lives out in Surrey. To catch the train there, I walked from my flat in Bloomsbury to Farringdon Station. My route took me, unsuspecting, down Hatton Garden. It was unusually quiet. Seventy per cent of the businesses were Jewish. The day before had been Passover and their shops were closed for the holiday weekend.

That particular Sunday I would certainly not have taken my other possible route – that was to take a bus from Southampton Row to Waterloo Station to catch the train there. A few days before, there had been a mysterious underground fire in Kingsway. The street was closed off and the buses had been diverted.

As I strolled through the heart of London's jewellery district on the morning of 5 April 2015, I cannot say I noticed anything suspicious, though just a metre or so beneath my feet there was a ransacked strongroom and a hole in the wall of a vault, whose shape has since become iconic.

The police famously had not noticed anything suspicious either. Two days earlier, the burglar alarm had gone off in the building. The police were informed, but decided not to investigate. They were, after all, busy directing traffic away from the scene of the fire in Kingsway, half a mile away.

The building's security guard, Kelvin Stockwell, was roused from his bed when the alarm went off in the early hours of Good Friday, 3 April. Arriving at the building, he took a look around but saw nothing amiss. Though the crooks were hard at work below street level, the basement appeared secure, so Kelvin went home.

Local residents were well accustomed to the sound of drilling and vibration. Crossrail were tunnelling from Holborn Station, near the Kingsway fire, under Hatton Garden to Farringdon Station, a hundred yards further on. The company had sent out letters warning locals about the tunnelling and the demolition work needed to make way for the new ticket hall at Farringdon so no one thought anything of it and the burglary was not reported until Hatton Garden opened for business again on the Tuesday morning. By then, the burglars had been home, basking in their good fortune, for two days.

Scotland Yard issued a statement saying: 'At approximately 08.10 hours today, Tuesday 7 April, police were called to a report of a burglary at a safety deposit business at Hatton Garden, EC1. The Flying Squad is investigating and detectives are currently at the scene. It appears that heavy cutting equipment has been used to get into a vault at the address, and a number of safety deposit boxes have been broken into.'

At the time the size of the heist was still unclear.

'We are still trying to establish exactly what has been stolen and who the losers are,' said one of the police at the scene. 'It was a chaos inside.'

Insurers said it would be some time before the true extent of the losses was known but no one had been hurt. The police appeared clueless. It seemed like the perfect heist.

'No dealer would be foolish to leave all their stock in one place,' a London diamond dealer observed, 'but even if they left a fraction of the uncut and semi-polished diamonds and other stones in a single box, the value could easily run into millions for one box alone.'

Local jeweller, Norman Bean, who had stored around £35,000 of jewellery there, upbraided Kelvin Stockwell.

'I came down and spoke to a security guard,' he recalled. 'He said he came on Friday, the alarm was going off. He went downstairs, looked through the door, through the windows, and couldn't see anything and came out again. That was it.

'I said, "Well, why didn't you open up and have a look in?" He told me he doesn't get paid enough. They could have been there all weekend. Who knows? It's a disgrace. It's like something out of a film. I can't believe it could happen.'

Defending his actions later, Kelvin Stockwell said: 'You don't know what you're going to walk into. You can't take that chance. Because I could have walked in, I don't know what would have happened to me. I could have been clumped across the head or got tied up, whatever. That's why the policy was you don't go in on your own. You wait and hopefully if the police turn up, you can go in with them.'

But, of course, they didn't.

It was then discovered that the same high-security depository had been raided thirteen years earlier when a thief posing as a customer emptied a number of safe deposit boxes. This time the haul was worth some £500,000. The Hatton Garden Safe Deposit Company had also been robbed in 1975, when armed robbers burst in, threatened staff and made off with an estimated £1.5 million in gems, cash and other valuables.

In the first reports of the Hatton Garden heist, it was thought that the haul might beat the estimated £60 million stolen from the Knightsbridge Security Deposit Centre in July 1987, where Italian armed robber Valerio Viccei requested to rent a deposit box. He and an accomplice then pulled guns, subdued the staff, broke into the boxes and made off. While other gang members were soon rounded up, Viccei fled the UK, though the fact that he had left behind one bloody fingerprint assured the Metropolitan Police that he was the ringleader.

With safety deposit box heists, it is impossible to get an accurate figure for the haul. No one but the depositor knows what is in the box. Sometimes they will contain valuables, dubiously obtained or being kept hidden from the authorities, that the owner will not admit to. Then there are other owners who might seize the opportunity to inflate the value of the contents of their box to make a dodgy insurance claim.

The Knightsbridge heist certainly rivalled the burglary of the Banco Central of Fortaleza in Brazil in 2005, where thieves spent three months tunnelling under two city blocks, then through three-and-a-half feet of reinforced concrete to steal some US$72 million in currency. Even this was small beer compared with the most lucrative bank robbery in history, where former Iraqi dictator Saddam Hussein's son Qusay made off with $920 million from the Central Bank of Iraq in 2003.

But when it came to safety deposit box heists, it was thought that Hatton Garden would top the polls. Former Flying Squad chief Roy Ramm said: 'I would not be surprised, given where this one is, in Hatton Garden, if £200 million is around the amount stolen.'

But we may never know.

'The amount of money and the goods that are taken is never fully revealed,' he added, 'and there's a good chance that not everybody would declare.'

However, he told BBC Radio Four's *Today* programme: 'There's a sort of old-fashioned audacity about it.'

CHAPTER TWO

DIAMOND GEEZERS

Although the haul in Hatton Garden did not approach £200 million, it did make the record books as the biggest raid in UK history, not that other villains had not tried bigger heists. In November 2000, the police had foiled a gang who tried to steal £350 million in diamonds by ram-raiding the De Beers diamond exhibition at the Millennium Dome using a JCB digger. This led to the classic *Sun* headline: 'I'm Only Here For De Beers'.

The raid, planned by three local Jack the Lads, was right out of a James Bond movie. The Millennium Jewels collection on display included the Millennium Star, a 203-carat, flawless gem that was considered one of the most perfect in the world, as well as eleven other priceless blue diamonds. Those jewels had played a central role in the spectacular laser light show that took place in the Dome during the Millennium festivities.

However, the Flying Squad was well ahead of the crooks. In the summer of 2000, they received a tip-off that a major armed robbery was being planned, and set up Operation Magician to collate intelligence. A failed £10-million robbery in Nine Elms in February 1999 had come to their attention. Robbers had welded a huge metal spike to the chassis of a lorry, covering it with the foliage of a discarded Christmas tree. The idea was to have been to drive it into a security van trapped at a roadblock, splitting open the doors, but the plan went awry when an irate motorist late for work removed the keys from the unattended vehicle. Thwarted, the crooks made off in an inflatable speedboat towards Chelsea.

'What that day did was inform me that there was a gang with a sufficient organisation and capability to carry off a robbery of an intense magnitude,' said Detective Chief Superintendent Jon Shatford.

A second attempt to skewer a security van was made in Aylesford, Kent, on 7 July 2000. It was foiled when a police car turned up unexpectedly. The robbers loosed off several shots before, again, making off in an inflatable.

The police tracked some of the vehicles used in this raid to two isolated farms in rural Kent, which were immediately put under 24-hour surveillance. By then officers had also received a tip-off about a raid on the Dome from an informer whose identity remains a closely-guarded secret but was thought to be an associate of notorious criminal Kenneth Noye, who was convicted for his involvement in the 1983 Brink's-Mat robbery, where £26 million of gold bullion, diamonds and cash was stolen from a warehouse at Heathrow.

'Most of the Brink's-Mat gold went through the Hatton Garden area,' said Brian Boyce, the senior detective on the case.

Noye was caught at his home in Kent and eventually convicted of handling some of the stolen bullion. When melting it down and recasting it, he is thought to have mixed in some copper coins to disguise the source.

While his home was under surveillance, Noye and an accomplice found Detective Constable John Fordham in the grounds spying on them. Noye stabbed Fordham eleven times, killing him. However, as Fordham was wearing a balaclava, Noye claimed at his trial in December 1985 that he did not realise the intruder was a police officer and he had acted in self-defence. He was acquitted.

After Fordham's death, his colleagues found eleven gold bars wrapped in red-and-white cloth hidden in a shallow gully beside Noye's garage wall. Back in court in 1986, Noye was sentenced to fourteen years for handling stolen bullion, serving eight. Later, he was given a life sentence for the road-rage murder of twenty-one-year-old motorist Stephen Cameron in 1996.

In September 2000, two months before the raid, forty-year-old Raymond 'Black Ray' Betson, of Chatham, Kent – thought to be the mastermind – and his forty-nine-year-old right-hand man William Cockram, from Catford, South-East London, were caught on film visiting the Dome.

At a meeting of detectives hunting the Nine Elms robbers, a detective inspector who had recently visited the Dome quipped: 'Maybe they are after the Millennium Jewels?'

'Christ, that's it,' cried another.

Once the penny had dropped, more than a hundred officers from the Flying Squad were placed on constant standby, backed up by armed officers.

'What I did not know – and I never knew until it happened – was how they were going to do it,' said Shatford.

The gang planned to lead the charge with a JCB, figuring the digger would not attract attention as there was plenty of building work going on in the vicinity. Once again the escape would be made by 55-mph speedboat. Russian gangsters were waiting in the Mayflower pub three minutes across the river in Rotherhithe to receive the stolen jewels. It was thought they were acting for a wealthy client, possibly an Arab.

The gang used pay-as-you-go mobile phones to arrange meetings. Known as 'burners', these could be disposed of after compromising calls to hinder surveillance. Members even posed as tourists with their families to film the diamonds in the Dome's Money Zone. It was noted that their frequent visits were always at high tide and Cockram and Betson were seen filming the nearby jetty and the river.

The villains were nothing short of audacious. Gang member Terry Millman, who died of cancer while awaiting trial, used the name 'T. Diamond' when he handed over £3,700 in cash to buy the getaway speedboat at a yard in the seaside town of Whitstable, Kent. The men were spotted testing it in a harbour in Kent. Ammonia gas was purchased, perhaps to knock out any potential have-a-go heroes, and smoke bombs bought to cause chaos. Equipment was stored in a disused commercial yard in Plumstead, South-East London, and two remote Kent farms near Maidstone.

The raid was planned for 6 October, but had to be called off after the speedboat developed engine problems. A month later, on 6 November, the second attempted was aborted when they miscalculated the tide. But the following day everything was set.

Shortly after 9 a.m., the JCB crashed through the perimeter and the side wall of the Dome's Money Zone. Four gang members dressed in body armour and gas masks leapt from the digger and went about their business. As the crowds were dispersed by smoke bombs, the gang faced their most formidable challenge yet – the diamonds' display cases, which were believed to be impregnable. They were built to resist the force of a 60-ton ram raid. The explosive-resistant glass was also designed to foil any known tool for at least thirty minutes. But Cockram believed he had the answer: he would weaken the glass with three shots from a powerful Hilti nail gun. Then Robert Adams would use a sledgehammer to smash the glass once it had been 'warmed'.

As Adams broke through, the plan appeared to be working to perfection. They were just 27 seconds away from seizing the world's most fabulous collection of diamonds.

'I was twelve inches from pay day,' Adams later recalled. 'It would have been a blinding Christmas!'

In fact, the diamonds had been replaced by replicas, with the originals stored elsewhere. Also, Dome staff had been replaced with armed undercover officers. Forty armed officers from the Specialist Firearms Command, SC&O19, were hidden behind a dummy wall. Sixty armed Flying Squad officers were stationed along the north bank of the Thames, with a further twenty on the river itself. Their commanding officers were in the Dome's CCTV room, watching while the cameras captured every moment of the drama as an army of police officers swooped.

As one member of the gang ruefully put it: 'We would have got away with it but for the fact there were 140 police waiting for us.'

The Dome's executive chairman, David James, arrived on the scene shortly after the men were arrested.

'They were all on the ground, trussed up like Christmas turkeys,' he said. 'It was relatively calm and they were almost joking with the police, who were standing over them with guns. About 150 yards away in the central area there were ninety-six

Miss World contestants taking a photocall – this was Monty Python stuff.'

Shatford said that it had been decided to wait until the gang had reached the diamonds before arresting them.

'Our chief concern throughout was public safety,' he said. 'We decided it was better to let the robbers get to the vault, where they were effectively imprisoned.'

When the trial opened at the Old Bailey, Cockram said: 'I couldn't believe how simple it was. I was thinking, this cannot be true; it was a gift. At first I had thought it was pie in the sky, but after going down there, I couldn't believe security was so bad. There was nobody in the vault, no security workers walking around.'

Had the plan succeeded, he said: 'It would have taken a very short time from hitting the main gate to getting back across the Thames – five minutes maximum.'

In his defence he added 'No one was going to get hurt – there was no one to hurt. The Dome was always empty.'

It was an old-fashioned crime that depended for its success on guile, audacity and high-tech Hilti equipment. The nail gun was to be used to break the glass, not to hurt anyone; the ammonia was to contaminate any traces of blood they might have left and the body armour was worn to protect them after the raid, when they were to have met 'Tony' and his associates across the river to exchange the gems for cash.

'We never trusted them,' Cockram admitted. 'They shoot people for anything these days. We thought we could be double-crossed – well, we *were* double-crossed, weren't we?'

Betson tried to blame his brother-in-law, serving police officer PC Michael Waring, who was working at the Dome as part of the perimeter security. Waring, he said, had told him about a school friend named Tony, who was also working at the Dome and had come up with a plan for the heist. Betson claimed that he had confidence in Tony's plan because the introduction had come through Waring.

'He had a backer – someone to buy the jewellery,' Betson explained. 'He said the security was crap. I had every confidence in him. There was no way I thought he would betray me, not for two seconds. If this had come to me from someone else – in a pub – I would not have gone along with it, but it was the background to where it had come from. It was solid.'

He had every confidence in Waring too.

'I did not think he would try and do me any harm,' Betson added. 'I trusted him.'

Cockram also confirmed that Betson had told him he had inside information.

'He said he had inside help through PC Michael Waring,' said Cockram.

PC Waring totally denied he was part of the plan or had offered to act in a criminal way by providing information on security. He was exonerated.

James Hurley, thought to be the mastermind behind the heist, was eventually traced to his hideout on the Costa del Sol. Meanwhile, Cockram and Betson got eighteen years each. Speedboat driver Kevin Meredith from Brighton was jailed for five years, while Lee Wenham was given four years, along with another nine years for the attempted robbery in Aylesford, which he also admitted.

Aldo Ciarrocchi, of Bermondsey, South-East London, and Robert Adams, of no fixed address, got fifteen years each. Adams, a cocaine smuggler who had served six years in the 1970s for trying to murder his first wife, had stayed outside the Dome vault, throwing smoke bombs to shield the other robbers, and planned to use the £50,000 he was promised for the raid to start a new life in America with his middle-class fiancée, twenty-five-year-old US model Elisabeth Kirsch, who said she had no idea he was a criminal.

Coincidentally, Ciarrocchi belonged to Britain's most notorious crime dynasty – the North London's Adams family, aka 'the A-Team', who have amassed a vast fortune through drugs and money laundering. Based in Clerkenwell, the Adams family has made Hatton Garden the centre of much of their activities. Indeed, they even have an office there.

CHAPTER THREE

HATTON GARDEN

Home to the UK's diamond trade, Hatton Garden is a terraced stretch of old Clerkenwell on the border of the City that has been the centre of London's jewellery trade since medieval times. It is no accident that Hatton Garden is also intelligence officer James Bond's first port of call in *Diamonds Are Forever*.

Ex-Flying Squad Detective Chief Inspector Peter Kirkham said of Hatton Garden: 'There is nowhere else in the UK, and only half a dozen places around the world, where you get such a concentration of diamonds. And they are small, easy to grab, carry, conceal and smuggle.'

Originally established by Jews fleeing persecution, the jewellery business in Hatton Garden received a boost at the end of the nineteenth century when South African mining giant De Beers chose London as its principal sales outlet. Pogroms in Eastern Europe and the rise of the Nazis brought Jewish refugees, who still dominate the trade. Formally or informally excluded from other trades and professions, many Jewish people gravitated towards the world of gems and precious metals. Fears of a rise in anti-Semitism also made it an attractive sector. As one Hatton Garden veteran put it: 'When you're persecuted, you need something you can carry. You can't carry a house in your pocket.'

Still around a third of the dealers in Hatton Garden are Jewish and on the street Yiddish is interspersed with Cockney rhyming slang. Modern-day criminals also found that the proceeds of crime, once converted into precious stones, are easily carried across borders.

'It is much easier to put a few thousand pounds in diamonds into a suitcase and take it across a border than it is to do the same thing with the cash equivalent,' said money-laundering expert Peter Lilley, author of *Dirty Dealing: The Untold Truth About Global Money Laundering, International Crime and Terrorism.*

The gold and silver content of stolen jewellery is easily converted into gold bullion and complex VAT scams can reap millions. When Mrs Thatcher came to power as Britain's first female Prime Minister in 1979, she scrapped VAT on the purchase of gold coins such as Krugerrands. This inadvertently created a golden opportunity for fraudsters as VAT continued to be imposed on the sale of gold bullion. Unscrupulous gold dealers would buy Krugerrands from the banks, melt them down and sell the resulting ingots back to the banks as gold bullion, adding VAT in the process, which they had no intention of passing on to the taxman. This process became even more lucrative as VAT was raised from 8 per cent to 15 per cent in 1979. This meant that on every transaction of £100,000, for example, they would make an additional profit of £15,000.

The banks would then legitimately reclaim the 15 per cent

VAT they paid out on the purchase of the gold. Consequently, the Exchequer lost out on revenue and effectively subsidised the fraud. Criminal gangs that had previously specialised in the dangerous business of armed robbery moved into this 'white-collar' crime, with Hatton Garden at the heart of this new illicit industry.

Customs and Excise eventually got wise to the scam and legislation was passed, re-imposing VAT on Krugerrands, but the crooks simply sourced their gold sovereigns from the Continent, where VAT was low or non-existent and carried on as before. It was estimated that frauds of this sort funnelled £1 billion of VAT money into criminal hands.

These days the gem trade appeals particularly to money launderers because, as banking regulations get ever tighter, it is one of the few remaining industries where large cash transactions can be carried out with complete anonymity.

'It is all based on trust so there is no paper trail,' Lilley explained. 'There is an environment of almost complete secrecy and it is a very cash-intensive marketplace. These are all things that money launderers find very attractive.'

Diamond-mounter Michael Lynton told the *Jewish Chronicle*: 'Everyone knows everyone. We give our word on deals. You stick by your word. If you don't, you're not considered a gentleman. If we had a load of paperwork there would be complete chaos.'

There are some 350 businesses and 55 shops in the area dealing in jewellery and gems. These sit on a honeycomb of underground tunnels, abandoned railway lines, decommissioned bunkers, ancient passageways thought to have been built by the monks of Ely, who once occupied nearby Ely Place, and the tributaries of London's second-largest river, the Fleet, which still flows through the sewer under Farringdon Road created by Queen Victoria's chief engineer of London's Metropolitan Board of Works Sir Joseph Bazalgette. Those who know the area well are amazed that it does not cave in.

Above this submerged city there is a labyrinth of concealed rooms. Along with the heavily guarded underground vaults filled with safety deposit boxes, there are stores of gold and silver and steel-lined workshops, where specialist items are made to order by master craftsmen. There are secure basements, where goldsmiths work, and small, locked rooms off dark stairwells, where diamond merchants sit examining glittering stones. These are protected by the latest high-tech equipment and security systems. Access is only open to those in the trade. You have to be recognised on the CCTV monitor to get through the first of a series of steel doors, then each in turn has to be locked before the next one opens.

Despite the dubious history of the Garden, gentrification has started to encroach. On a Saturday afternoon you are more likely to meet couples looking for engagement rings than dodgy spivs with bulging coat pockets. But some of the old characters remain and with its wares displayed behind armoured glass widows, it still attracts criminals so the traders club together to hire two burly Russian private security guards, who stand conspicuously at either end of the street. Other less conspicuous men, mainly ex-military Eastern Europeans, keep watch on street corners, the ridges of their bulletproof vests only faintly visible under their black T-shirts. They know everything that goes on in the street, keeping in touch by radio earpieces. The dealers also operate a closed shop.

'Somebody screws over a dealer, say, you won't do it again,' said one. 'Your picture will be faxed to everyone else within minutes.'

It is estimated that around £1 billion in jewels passes through the Garden every year. So, for the sake of security, the traders there like to keep their stock in safety deposit boxes overnight and on public holidays – plainly a prime target for any self-respecting criminal.

The burglars in the Hatton Garden diamond heist had clearly done their homework. When the police turned up on 7 April 2015, they quickly deduced that the villains had got down to the basement via a lift shaft, disabled the alarms from the inside and tunnelled their way into the vault using heavy-duty cutting tools, which they had left behind.

Clients of the company were clearly frustrated.

'I am relying on them. It is a joke,' said one dealer. 'How could someone bring all that heavy equipment in?'

His family has had a safety deposit box with the company for around thirty years.

'It has happened three times now,' he explained. 'If my safe is all right, I am taking it out of there. My father had a box there and it is the second time since I have had one.'

The press quickly drew a comparison between the raid and the film *Sexy Beast*, starring Ben Kingsley and Ray Winstone, where a gang target a London safe deposit centre. Criminals who steal from safety deposit boxes also benefit from the slightly ambivalent public reaction to such thefts, one newspaper noted, as most people suspected that some of the victims may have been hiding ill-gotten gains themselves, whether from the police, the taxman or the ex-wife.

'It's a well-planned job. They picked the right time considering everyone was away over the holidays,' said gem wholesaler Mohammad Shah.

Easter gave the robbers up to four days to go about their business uninterrupted. The previous robbery there had taken place at Christmas.

'I had hundreds of thousands worth in there,' said Shah, who rented a safe deposit box. 'It's insured but some is very rare and I won't be able to replace it.'

Others were also on tenterhooks. The police had sealed off the building and no one knew what was missing.

'Everybody wants to know what has been taken but the police are not telling us anything,' added Shah. 'I am waiting to find out. They said they could maybe tell me tomorrow. I am insured, but many people who use these boxes are not. The truth is nobody really knows what is kept in these boxes.'

Another jeweller, who wished to be unnamed, said: 'You are looking at tens and tens of millions, maybe hundreds of millions. This could be devastating for many people whose livelihoods depend on dealing with jewellery. They will have insurance, but you can't operate without stock.'

One dealer revealed he kept forty years' worth of stock in there. Another said a typical box contained valuables worth around £250,000. Some put the losses even higher. One jeweller who had worked in the area for two decades said: 'I'd guess each box contained about £500,000, possibly more.'

But no one could be sure. With jewellery and gems locked in safety deposit boxes, the Hatton Garden Safe Deposit Company kept no record of the contents. Clients pay around £300 for a medium-sized box and must give their name and address, and produce identification, but they do not have to say what is in the box. Boxes were opened in private rooms where there were no cameras, so owners can keep anything, from piles of cash or jewels to firearms, in them.

'When you go down into a vault it really is just like a James Bond movie,' said Neil Duttson, a diamond dealer who buys stones for private clients and travels with his own bodyguard when carrying expensive gems. 'It is a secure steel vault – a room lined with hundreds of boxes. People can keep absolutely anything: it could be a new Rolex, it could be a family heirloom, but for most around here it will be the tools of their business.'

Most of the victims were small, independent businesses and workshop owners who did not have their own safes and used the boxes to store their stock overnight. Many admitted that they were not insured as they waited for the police to confirm whose boxes had been emptied.

Jerry Landon, a Hatton Garden trader for almost fifty years, had recently put jewellery worth hundreds of thousands into two boxes in the vault as he was due to go into hospital for a knee operation.

'I still haven't heard anything,' he said. 'The whole situation is very distressing.'

The Garden was a close-knit community and everybody would have their say. Tony Dellow, a denizen of Hatton Garden since 1976, had a jewellery workshop on the second floor of a brick building opposite the depository but he kept his stock in a huge safe painted in the colours of West Ham Football Club. He had not been affected by the raid, but said it had 'devastated' the street.

'It is all done on trust here,' he explained. 'Everything works on a very informal basis. Deals are done on the shake of a hand and your word is your bond. That is how we are.'

Michael Miller, a jeweller from Knightsbridge, London, admitted he 'felt sick' at the prospect of losing up to £50,000 of jewellery and watches that were uninsured.

'I can't believe this actually happened,' he said. 'I have a collection of watches I was going to give my son and that is irreplaceable. I bought an IWC GST Aquatimer on the day my son was born and I was going to give it to him when he turns eighteen. They don't make them any more.'

Miller had held a deposit box with the company for almost ten years and said many jewellers in the area used the firm to store their stock at the end of the day. He estimated some boxes could contain valuables worth up to £2 million.

'If you look at their website, they say they are the safest place around,' he added. 'There is a double-door entry and a locked system to go in. You have to go through two doors to get in the place and then get into the vault.'

Indeed, the company's website boasted that it was 'one of London's most successful and leading safe deposit companies'. It promised to 'protect important and irreplaceable personal belongings' and carried the slogan: 'Clients' Safety: We Can Guarantee It'.

That seemed like an empty promise now.

Miller was even more perturbed when he discovered that the alarm went off, but the police did not turn up.

'I am just so shocked and disappointed to hear the police didn't answer that alarm,' he said. 'I mean, before, we thought maybe the police didn't even know about that, but now we know that they knew something was wrong. This completely changes things, the knowledge that something could have been done. The police pride themselves on being somewhere in a couple of minutes, but on this occasion they just weren't there.'

A store owner near the scene said: 'It's just shocking that someone didn't answer that call that came in when the alarm went off. You think, what on earth isn't a high priority call if it isn't a safe deposit alarm going off in there? I know they're investigating, but really, what is the good of that when the damage is done? There are people who will have lost their livelihoods because of this.'

Scotland Yard issued a statement explaining what had happened. It said:

> At this stage we have established that on Friday, 3 April at 00:21hrs a call was received at the MPS Central Communications Command (MetCC) from Southern Monitoring Alarm Company. The call stated that a confirmed intruder alarm had been activated at the Hatton Garden Safe Deposit Ltd. The call was recorded and transferred to the police's CAD (computer aided despatch) system. A grade was applied to the call that meant that no police response was deemed to be required. We are now investigating why this grade was applied to the call. This investigation is being carried out locally. It is too early to say if the handling of the call would have had an impact on the outcome of the incident.

The Met said they heard about the burglary when they were called at around 8.10 a.m. on the Tuesday morning. Calls to the Met's central communications command are initially dealt with by a 'first contact' operator, who grades all incidents 'in terms of their urgency,' according to the force's website:

> Upon receiving a call, information is recorded and passed on to the relevant department, or to a dispatcher for a police deployment if required. First contact operators will question the caller and gain all the relevant information necessary to ensure the best police response. Having completed this, the operator will grade the call in accordance with standard operating

procedures for the type of incident. The grading will depend upon the urgency of the call.

Plainly, the call on the Tuesday morning, unlike the alarm on Friday night, was graded urgent. Soon they were confirming that goods were missing, including a box containing a £40,000 diamond, platinum, gold and other diamonds worth between £5,000 and £10,000 – worth in all £150,000, according to the owner's brother. It was uninsured.

'I'm very angry. It's my brother's life down there and the worst thing is we don't know what's happened,' he said. 'You would imagine the police would come straight away, wouldn't you, on a street like this? It's absolutely ridiculous. That place should have been wired to the police straight away. It's all going to come out, isn't it? But that doesn't help us. We're in limbo and struggling.'

In fact, the police drew criticism from all quarters. Another dealer, who has been a diamond and gem trader for forty years, noted sarcastically: 'It's not important enough, it's only two million . . . but don't worry about it.'

While some found out early on whether they had lost out, others endured an agonising wait.

'The robbery was reported on Tuesday but by Friday we had still not been told whether our stuff had been taken,' said one jeweller. 'I had £350,000 worth of cash and jewels and I was in a terrible state.'

Some resorted to bribing security guards to find out what had been lost.

'By Friday, some of us owners had had enough and each paid the staff at the building £100 to have a look at the list of boxes missing,' said a lucky one. 'Mine was fine, but a friend had his life savings completely stolen, worth £500,000.'

Anger centred on the police's failure to follow up the alarm, giving the robbers the long Easter weekend to go about their business. The cash-strapped Met were soon threatened with action for millions in compensation.

'As far as I'm concerned, the police have got a lot to answer for,' said one victim. 'Suing anyone is a last resort but it's something I would consider.'

In fact, there was no prospect of the police facing out a multimillion-pound compensation bill for their failure to safeguard the building.

Graeme Trudgill, executive director of the British Insurance Brokers' Association, said: 'When you look at case law the police have immunity. It is very difficult to see how it could be proved that they have breached their duty of care. The key question is whether the Hatton Garden Safety Deposit Company had a specific contract with the alarm company and the details of that contract. Has there been a breach of contract on the part of the security firm or the police? In terms of suing the police, a law firm would look at past evidence and see how difficult that could be.'

Diamond dealer Neil Duttson spotted fresh difficulties. He said that tracing any gems stolen in the heist would be nearly impossible.

'Once diamonds have been re-cut and polished, there is no geological map,' he explained. He also believed that the thieves would wait for some months before acting.

'I imagine they will be sat on for six months,' he said, adding wryly, 'You can expect some cheap diamonds will be coming on the market soon.'

While the safe deposit employed its own security guards, the whole of the jewellery quarter was patrolled by Hatton Garden

Security Limited. Its director, Darren Boorman, said his staff had not noticed anything untoward over the Easter weekend.

CHAPTER FOUR

INSIDE JOB?

Newspapers quickly speculated that the heist must have been an inside job, pointing out that, while planning the Knightsbridge Security Deposit heist, Valerio Viccei, then wanted for more than fifty armed robberies in Italy, befriended the managing director of the centre, Parvez Latif, a known cocaine user, who was heavily in debt. A bloody fingerprint had tied Viccei to the crime. While the rest of the gang were rounded up, Viccei fled to Latin America, but he returned soon after to retrieve his Ferrari Testarossa. He was then caught in a roadblock, where the police smashed the front window of his car and dragged him out.

'All right, the game is up and you have no need to be nasty,' he observed, stoically. 'You are the winners, so calm down and everything is going to be fine.'

Sentenced to twenty-two years in jail, Viccei was deported after five to serve out the rest of his time in an Italian jail. In

2000, while on day release, he got into a gunfight with police and was killed.

Looking for clues, *The Guardian* also recalled the £53-million robbery that took place at the Securitas depot in Tonbridge, Kent, in 2006. There was an inside man too – Albanian Emir Hysenaj, who had briefly worked at the centre, had filmed inside it with a hidden camera. In the building at 88–90 Hatton Garden, the paper decided that, once the burglars had gained entry, there were 'a million places to hide' until it closed for the Easter weekend.

The Eastern European outfit that had carried out the so-called 'Pink Panther' robberies were among the suspects. They were a gang of Serbs, Montenegrins and Bosniaks, possibly veterans of the war in the former Yugoslavia, who first came to attention in 1993 when they stole a diamond worth £500,000 from a jeweller in London's New Bond Street. It was later found hidden a jar of face cream, a ploy borrowed from the *Pink Panther* films.

The gang seems to have as many as 60 members, who have been responsible for over 120 robberies in some twenty countries. In Dubai, in 2008, they used black-and-white Audi limousines to speed across the polished floors of an upmarket shopping mall, before smashing in the front window of a jewellery shop. In Tokyo, in 2004, they took just 36 seconds to steal £2 million worth of gems from a store. Then, in 2013, one of their number was thought to have stolen jewels worth US$136 million from the Carlton International Hotel in Cannes, where Alfred Hitchcock set his 1955 film, *To Catch a Thief*. It was believed to have been the biggest jewellery heist of all time. French police also believe that they were responsible for the £6.4-million raid on two security lorries. Pink Panthers have been arrested periodically, but have escaped in daring prison breaks.

INSIDE JOB?

Former Flying Squad detective Jim Dickie said: 'I am sure the Flying Squad will be looking to see if there is a link with the Pink Panther Gang. Their priority would be to get uncut diamonds because it is much easier to cut them and sell them on. I think they would have had an inside agent because they knew the layout and where to drill. They could have had an expert in the vaults to examine the diamonds and other stones to see which were the most valuable.'

Gang members prided themselves on the artistry of their heists and their ability to disguise themselves. They had a sophisticated network of middlemen capable of re-setting stones and re-cutting them for sale on the black market and Scotland Yard said it would 'ask for assistance from other agencies here and in any other country'.

Speculation grew that the mastermind who had financed the Hatton Garden heist was of Eastern European origin. But Scott Selby, author of *Flawless*, an account of the $108-million diamond heist in Antwerp of 2003, discounted reports that the Pink Panthers were behind the raid.

'The Pink Panthers tend to use very fast, paramilitary-style violence,' he observed. 'This seems impressive and well-planned. I think it will be local British criminals.'

While the gang would largely have been unarmed, experts believed that one of their number would have carried a shotgun and acted as 'policeman'. A former Flying Squad officer said: 'His job would have been to watch their backs in case any police, guards or nosy members of the public turned up. The rest of the gang would have been hand-picked – including people who knew how to use the cutting equipment.'

Other skills were on hand.

'It's not hard to get rid of diamonds,' a retired jewel thief told

THE GREAT DIAMOND HEIST

The Guardian. 'They wouldn't need to take them to Switzerland, they could easily tuck them back into the trade here. Who could it be? Serbs? Who knows?'

Jewels were easier to get rid of than paintings or banknotes, he added. Diamonds, whether rough or polished, could be easily re-cut and sold on. The source was one of the first to speculate that the massive electrical fire in Kingsway before the break-in could have conveniently messed up the alarm system. Locals also complained that there had been a power cut immediately before the raid that might have given the criminals an opportunity to tamper with the alarms. The Kingsway fire cut had caused disruption throughout the area. In Covent Garden, the theatres had to park generators outside to keep their shows onstage.

Those living in the area were not shy about coming forward with information. Nineteen-year-old Farhana Begum, who lived in a flat just ten seconds' walk from the raided premises, said: 'My mum actually heard drilling on the Friday night, it was probably about 9 p.m. or 9.30 p.m. But there had been roadworks, or construction work, going on in the street for the last couple of weeks, so she thought that they may have been working late. But she did think it was quite weird that they would be drilling at that time. Also, the weekend before it happened, there was an electrical cut. It was over that weekend, so before the Holborn fire as well. It happened on either the Friday or the Saturday, it was just a bit peculiar.'

The student went on to explain: 'Monday to Friday during the day this area is buzzing. But after 5 p.m. and over the weekends it can be so quiet. I think most people would think this area has lots of high security and is busy all the time, so they must have known the area. We have had no communication from the police at all. They don't seem to have made any attempt to speak to us.'

There had been another robbery in Begum's street a few years earlier. Thieves had targeted Berganza Ltd, cutters and merchants of gemstones. The store was a matter of seconds away from the vault, around the corner on Greville Street.

'It's not the first time something like this has happened,' she said. 'There was an armed robbery at Berganza around three or four years ago as well. But I think they caught the person who did that.'

A woman who lived in a flat above a jeweller's in Hatton Garden said her husband also heard a loud noise on Good Friday.

'My husband said he heard a loud bang late on Friday night, but he wasn't sure what it was,' she revealed. 'We have no idea if it was connected or not. But this street used to be awful a few years ago. Alarms would go off on the Friday night and they would just continue all weekend. You would be ringing and ringing the police and they would never come out. All they would say is they're having problems contacting the key-holder.'

Data scientist John Han lived with Chenwei Zheng opposite the exit used by the thieves.

'I heard drilling late on Thursday but thought it was workmen after we had a huge power cut,' he told the press. The noise had gone on until the early hours of Good Friday.

'We had been out for dinner that night for my girlfriend's birthday. We did hear what sounded like drilling in the middle of the night but went back to sleep. I did think at the time: who the hell does drilling at this hour?'

They assumed the noise was connected to repair work in the area after another power blackout the previous weekend.

'When I heard the news, I realised it was the gang drilling into the vault,' he added.

The Guardian spotted the similarity between the Hatton Garden heist and another raid in Baker Street in 1971. There, a gang spent weekends tunnelling their way into the vault of Lloyds Bank that held safe deposit boxes. It was another robbery where the police were caught curiously slow on their feet.

The robbers had rented a leather-goods shop named Le Sac two doors from the branch of Lloyds on the corner of Baker Street and Marylebone Road and began tunnelling a distance of some 50 feet under the Chicken Inn restaurant in between. They worked only on weekends because of the noise.

The film *The Bank Job* was made about the raid. When it came out in 2008, the *Daily Mirror* tracked down one of the gang.

'Before we got started, myself and an accomplice dressed up in bowler hats and pinstripes and went into the bank,' he explained. 'We were able to measure out the distance from the wall to the vault using an umbrella so we could calculate how far we needed to tunnel and didn't end up popping up in the wrong place. The actual tunnelling took three weeks because we could only do it at the weekend so we wouldn't be heard by bank and shop staff. We would go back on Friday night and tunnel until Monday morning.'

They tunnelled under the Chicken Inn and then, using a thermal lance, tried to bore through the three feet of reinforced concrete which made up the vault floor.

'We were using the highest-powered drills and torches we could find at the time but they weren't powerful enough to get through the reinforced concrete,' the robber added. 'In the end we had to blast our way in with explosives.'

The concrete was not wired to the alarm system as it was

thought to be impenetrable. Eight tons of rubble were excavated and left behind.

'When we finally came up, I was unable to fit through the hole and could only stick my head in,' he added. 'But others got in and grabbed the boxes.'

The gang didn't have time to go through all of the stash and ended up taking some sensitive material.

'When we got out, we realised we had a lot more than we'd bargained for,' one of the raid members said. One of the boxes belonged to a top politician, now deceased. 'When we opened it, we dropped it on the floor like it was a time bomb. We didn't want to take anything that might give us extra trouble so we left it. All we wanted was cash and jewels.'

The robber refused to talk about some of the sensitive material they came across, rumoured to include pictures of Princess Margaret, then still married to Lord Snowdon, cavorting with naked men on the Caribbean island of Mustique.

'I can't talk about that. But we did find a lot of guns,' the robber said. 'What was most disturbing was the child pornography we found. We were disgusted and left it in their open boxes so police could trace the owners.'

The robbers spray-painted on the inside of the vault: 'Let Sherlock Holmes try to solve this'.

Indeed, comparisons were drawn between this robbery and one that Sherlock Holmes did solve in the story 'The Red-Headed League'. It was a 'three-pipe problem', where a red-haired pawn-broker is lured from his shop so that his assistant can tunnel through the basement wall into the vault of the bank in the next street.

The Baker Street blaggers made their breakthrough into the vault on the night of Saturday, 11 September. At around 11.15 p.m. amateur radio enthusiast Robert Rowlands, who lived on nearby Wimpole Street, was going to bed with a cup of tea and an Ian Fleming novel, when he switched on his radio and overheard a walkie-talkie conversation between a lookout on a roof overlooking the bank and one of the tunnellers.

'I was trying to tune into Radio Luxembourg,' he explained. But instead, he found himself listening to a man with a strong South London accent, saying: 'We've got about 400,000. We'll let you know when we're coming out. Can you hear me?'

The reply came: 'I can hear you, how long do you think you're going to be in there, then?'

'I knew any robbery had to be within a mile-and-a-half radius of my flat to pick up a signal,' added Rowlands, 'and I thought it was taking place in a tobacconist shop – 400,000 cigarettes seemed the most likely theft.'

When he called the local police station a sarcastic officer said if he 'heard any more funny voices' he should record them. So he did, on a cassette-tape machine he was using to teach himself Spanish. Shortly after midnight, a man called Steve told the lookout: 'We want you to mind it for one hour from now, and then stop there, and go off air, and then come back on the air with both radios at six o'clock in the morning, over.'

The lookout was concerned that the rest of the gang might want him to remain in place while they left for the night, but Steve told him: 'Look, the place is filled with fumes and if security come in and smell them we are all going to take stoppo [make a hasty getaway] and none of us have got nothing, whereas this way we've all got three hundred grand to cut up.'

Another gang member chipped in, telling the lookout: 'You can't go now, we're almost there.' However, the unequivocal response from the lookout was: 'Money may be your God, but it's not mine, and I'm f***ing off!'

In the end he relented, and agreed to remain on the rooftop overnight before signing off.

Rowlands called the local police again. This time a constable came round, but was called away after half an hour. In frustration, Rowlands then called Scotland Yard.

'The uniform branch don't know what they're doing,' he said, after two officers were sent over.

'They sat on chairs by my bed, and we stayed up all night,' he added.

By dawn another pair of plainclothes officers joined them round the radio for the Sunday morning instalment.

Eventually, at 9 a.m., Steve came back on air, telling the lookout: 'We're going to finish off in here and we shall be coming out early this afternoon and you'll just have to bluff, bluff your way straight down off the roof.'

The criminals were making their getaway and Rowlands was indignant.

'They'd had ten hours to locate the raid while it was happening, yet didn't take action until it was too late,' he declared.

Eventually a senior office called in a detector van in an attempt to trace the transmissions, but by the time engineers could be brought in from weekend leave, the walkie-talkie conversations had ceased. However, police knew the raid must have been taking place within a 10-mile radius of Rowland's flat on Wimpole Street. There were 750 banks in that area. On the Sunday afternoon, they visited the branch of Lloyds on the corner of Baker Street and Marylebone Road but found no sign of entry as the vault doors had been left intact. They were unaware the raiders were still inside. It was not until the bank opened for business after the weekend that the robbery was discovered.

The thieves got away with £1.5 million in cash, worth some £19 million today. Then there were the valuables from 260 safe deposit boxes, possibly worth that much again. Reporting of the theft was quickly curtailed. Fleet Street editors were leant on to drop the story and Rowland was instructed not to talk to the press.

When a reporter visited Rowlands the following morning to ask about his involvement, he was warned off by a detective.

'When they discovered the reporter was telling his editor about the story, they grabbed the phone and my recording, which I didn't get back for six years,' said Rowlands. He claims the police told the editor that there was a D-Notice on the story, banning publication.

The police threatened to prosecute Rowlands for listening to an unlicensed radio station, but he did receive a £2,500 reward from Lloyds. Rowlands believed that the police put the strong arm on him in an attempt to cover up their own incompetence, although there were rumours that more sinister machinations were afoot. It was rumoured that MI5 was involved because photographs in one of the boxes substantiated an affair between Princess Margaret, whose marriage to Lord Snowdon was on its last legs, and the black radical Michael X, then in custody for murder in Trinidad.

'He was untouchable while he had the photos,' explained film producer George McIndoe, who had been in touch with two of the gang. 'When the intelligence services found out where they were being kept, they put word out that the bank would be easy to rob.'

Michael X was convicted and hanged in Trinidad and Tobago in 1975. The file on him is closed until 2054.

There were also allegations that one of the boxes contained photographs showing a then-famous politician abusing children.

Gang members were disgusted; they were only interested in cash and jewels, but they left the images on the floor for the police to find in the hope that he would be exposed.

In January 1973 four men had been convicted of the 'walkie-talkie robbery', as it became known, at a trial at the Old Bailey. Anthony Gavin, thirty-eight, a photographer from Brownlow Road in Dalston; Thomas Gray Stephens, thirty-five, a car dealer from Maygood Street in Islington; and Reginald Samuel Tucker, thirty-seven, a company director from Lee Street in Hackney, all pleaded guilty and were sentence to twelve years' imprisonment, though Stephens's and Tucker's sentences were subsequently reduced to eight years on appeal. The fourth man, Benjamin Wolfe, sixty-six, a leather goods dealer from Dovercourt Road in East Dulwich, pleaded not guilty but was subsequently convicted and sentenced to eight years. Wolfe had signed the lease on the shop used by the robbers.

Two other men accused of handling banknotes from the robbery were acquitted. According to one press report, the police believed that the mastermind of the crime was another London car dealer, who was never apprehended. Most of the loot was never recovered either.

CHAPTER FIVE

JEWEL IN THE CROWN

According to its website, Hatton Garden Safe Deposit Ltd was founded in 1954, 'making it one of the first companies in the UK to offer safe deposit boxes'. It also claimed to be 'currently one of London's most successful and leading safe deposit companies aiming to provide our clients a secure and cost-effective solution to store and protect important and irreplaceable personal belongings'.

Owned by Mahendra and Manish Bavishi, the company extolled its 'modern technological security', claiming clients 'benefit from our vast experience in this business which enables us to cater to various needs of different individuals, namely long- or short-term rentals and various safe sizes, and along with flexible access and modern technological security it is obvious why we are the only choice for all our existing clients'. Given its location, it was used extensively by jewellery dealers who sell to shops on the street. Many gemstone dealers who supply the area's exclusive jewellery trade were known to use the company to store stones as well as jewellery pieces.

According to Companies House, sixty-nine-year-old Mahendra Bavishi was living in Khartoum in the Sudan, while thirty-eight-year-old Manish gave an address in Wembley, North London. In the aftermath of the robbery, he could not be contacted and a neighbour said he had not been seen since before Easter.

Meanwhile, a building worker sent in to assess the damage told the press: 'It was one hell of a mess. They could have been there for days. There is a lot of building work going on at the Crossrail project nearby so nobody would have thought any drilling was out of place.'

Another source close to the investigation said: 'They had plenty of time to carry this out. They had a lot of time on their hands and they knew what they were doing.'

The Met warned that its investigation would be 'a slow and painstaking process involving forensic examination, photographing the scene and recovering exhibits in meticulous detail in order to preserve the evidence'. It would take around two days. The police also had to study CCTV footage as the crooks might have rented safe deposit boxes under false names to study the security.

'Officers are working closely with Hatton Garden Safe Deposit Ltd to establish the identities of those affected,' said a spokesman. 'Police will be contacting victims directly.'

Fanciful stories about how the thieves had gained access soon circulated. Newspapers carried diagrams of them cutting through the roof, tunnelling their way through one wall and then through another into the lift shaft of the building. Using ropes, it was said that they abseiled down the shaft to the basement, smashed their way through a false wall and then cut through an 18-inch-thick metal door into the vault. They disarmed the sophisticated alarm and stole the CCTV system's hard drive before spending the bank holiday weekend drilling into security boxes and plundering their contents. Also, it was thought the thieves had hidden in the offices across the road, keeping the building under surveillance until the security guards had locked up on Thursday night. It was a plot straight out of *Mission Impossible*.

In the eyes of the police, this was the work of a seasoned gang who knew what they were doing. Ex-Flying Squad boss Barry Phillips told the press: 'This was a highly organised, sophisticated crime by a professional team and has all the hallmarks of a Hollywood film. It is inconceivable they would not have had inside help. The raid was well planned and well executed. They must have had inside information to be able to get into a premises like that, to know the routes, the vulnerabilities, the lift shaft, and to defeat a state-of-the-art security system. There are only a few criminals with the expertise to have done a job like this.'

He said the police would never know the true value of what was stolen due to the secretive nature of the safety deposit box industry. Besides, the loot was already on the move.

'It's likely the gems were already sourced and are now out of the country,' said Phillips. 'If past jobs like this are a guide, the thieves will have placed all of the jewellery prior to the robbery. That takes high organisation by the villains. But I think it's likely they'll let greed get the better of them and give themselves away.'

He thought that the gang would inevitably draw attention to themselves.

'They've got a vast amount of money. Splashing their cash

could lead to one of them giving the game away,' he explained. 'There's no honour among thieves. All it takes is for someone to get jealous. It can still go wrong.'

He also believed it was suspicious how they had breached the state-of-the-art security, adding: 'Very few would be able to finance and organise this. I can't recall a case of this kind that did not have an insider.'

But over the decades Hatton Garden has become a regular target for professional criminals. That's why the mostly Jewish traders have maintained their closed society.

'Everything is about trust,' said expert Rachel Lichtenstein, author of *Diamond Street*. 'It operates like a village, a very old-fashioned world where everybody knows each other and some people still speak in Yiddish. Deals are still sealed with a handshake and your face is still known – if you're not known, people won't deal with you. When you go behind the scenes there's an almost Dickensian feel to some of the ways business operates, but security is at a very high level. When you're working with diamonds, that's the way it has to be.'

Traditionally, deals were sealed in the small kosher cafés that once populated the area with the Yiddish expression '*Mazel und broche*' – 'luck and blessing'. That would never happen now. However, even during the investigation, a dealer in his thirties was seen counting out thousands of pounds in £20 notes under a table in a coffee shop to pay for a watch before driving off in a Mercedes.

The links between Hatton Garden and the criminal underworld had been highlighted in violent fashion in 1998, when local diamond merchant, Solly Nahome, was gunned down outside his North London home. A professional hitman pumped four bullets into him before escaping on a waiting motorcycle. It was a hit with all the hallmarks of the A-Team, London's most vicious criminal enterprises led by fearsome Terry Adams – Hatton Garden is on their patch.

After the gang graduated from protection rackets to armed robbery and drug running, they based themselves in London's gem quarter, where they could work closely with the sort of people who were in a good position to launder their ill-gotten millions.

In addition to having a business in Hatton Garden, Solly Nahome was a specialist in fraud and money laundering, as well as being the A-Team's trusted financial adviser. Recruited by Patsy Adams, the gang's enforcer, he was said to have met with members of the Adams family two or three times a week and arranged for £25 million to be hidden in property deals and offshore accounts.

Like other characters associated with the Adams family, Nahome tried to live below the radar. His name did not appear on the electoral register and he preferred to pay for everything in cash. The cash-only environment of Hatton Garden was the perfect place for laundering drugs money. It subsequently emerged that one of Osama bin Laden's top lieutenants had visited Hatton Garden in the run-up to the 9/11 attacks to raise funds for al-Qaeda.

Before his death, Nahome was said to have been on a number of trips abroad, including one visit to Israel, for business deals connected with the Adams family. He also opened a bar-restaurant near Hatton Garden as a front for their interests.

'Hatton Garden has a number of people whose history is not exactly squeaky clean,' said local jeweller Joel Grunberger, who worked with film director Guy Ritchie on his diamond-heist thriller *Snatch* (2000). 'Honest dealers work cheek-by-jowl with the villains. I don't mean that they sell to the villains but within the businesses, there are unscrupulous people.'

THE GREAT DIAMOND HEIST

When more than $100 million of gems were stolen in Antwerp in 2003, Grunberger reckoned, 'Some of the diamonds are certain to end up in London . . . Everyone knows the Brink's-Mat gold haul came to Hatton Garden.'

Gold worth more than £500 million from the 1983 robbery at Heathrow has never been recovered. Over the ensuing years some twenty people connected to that heist have been killed. A retired Flying Squad commander, John O'Connor, who investigated the Brink's-Mat robbery, feared a similar outcome from Hatton Garden raid.

'This type of robbery you will invariably get an awful lot of violence coming after it,' he says. 'Some of the gear in those deposit boxes is going to be owned by criminals and they will be looking for revenge.'

But some thieves do appear to get away with it. In June 2003 the contents of several security boxes were stolen from Hatton Garden Safe Deposit by a man calling himself Philip Goldberg or Luis Ruben – and sometimes Ruben Luis. In his mid-fifties, he dressed soberly like the other dealers and spent months ingratiating himself to local dealers. He bought diamonds for jewellers to examine and like the others, he regularly entered the grand stone doorway of 88–90 Hatton Garden.

The seven-storey building has marble floors, a lift and a spiral staircase. It accommodates about sixty businesses, including Persian gem dealers, watch traders and diamond wholesalers. Small studios, large enough for two craftsmen, rent for £10,000 a year. Like other street traders, he would disappear down the dark green linoleum staircase lit by dim fluorescent lights to the basement, where he had hired four strongboxes dotted around in the vault that measures just 15 feet square.

He made his last visit there at 9 a.m. on Saturday, 28 June. In retrospect that might have seemed a little suspicious. It was the Sabbath and Orthodox Jews were at home or in the synagogue, and for Saturday-morning shoppers it was a little early. CCTV footage showed him later walking out with a large black holdall. He has not been seen since.

The theft was not discovered until the Monday morning when a customer found his safety deposit box glued shut. At least £1.5 million in jewellery and cash was missing. No one could figure out how he had done it.

'If he could get away with it in the safety deposit, no lock in the world is safe,' said one dealer.

Clearly Goldberg/Ruben/Luis had built up trust in the Garden. Renting four boxes costing him some £900, he had good reason to hang around the safe depository, chatting with other clients.

'He offered stones to one or two of our members,' says Harry Levy, vice-president of the London Diamond Bourse, the city's most exclusive commodity exchange. 'There was this one particular large stone he was touting, but whether it was real, who knows? If he was using it as bait, he probably wouldn't show it too closely.'

But the actual mechanics of the theft were more of a mystery. To open a safe deposit box, you need two keys. The customer has one key; the staff hold another: it's the same for all boxes. A box can only be opened using both simultaneously. Even if the thief obtained a copy of the safe deposit's master key, he would still have to get copies of the individual keys of the boxes that he stole from. He did not appear to have used force and had he tried to use a mechanical or laser-powered device to cut through the tungsten and steel of the deposit boxes this would have been picked up by the CCTV cameras.

One theory was that he knocked a key out of a client or staff members' hand, as if by accident. Then, when he picked it up to give it back, he made a wax impression in his palm. Hypnosis was another possibility; he might even have been a magician.

'I'll never forget, my mother, years ago – she had a couple come in this shop to look at a very expensive diamond,' one veteran jeweller told *The Guardian*. 'Neither one of them touched it at any time. I was very nervous. We were all watching; we had a custodian in the corner who was watching. Then the man made my mother wrap the ring and seal it in tissue paper. They left the shop, saying they had to go and get the money. And then I had a horrible feeling. I made my mother open the package; she didn't want to, but in the end, she opened it. There was no ring. Eventually we got in touch with [magician] Paul Daniels. He told us there were a whole lot of ways it could have been done.'

Jim Hill, who worked with the organisation Trace, which helps police recover and identify stolen art and antiques, said: 'You're looking at an extremely clever locksmith. If there's no damage to the locks themselves, then he obviously has got keys made to fit each individual lock, but I'm just guessing the different methods.'

He said that he knew of only one similar theft in the UK and that was an inside job involving one of the guards. Generally, the Hatton Garden dealers had a sneaking respect for the culprit's calmness and audacity.

'Most of the stuff he took – diamonds – well, you can just put it in your pocket,' said dealer Jeffrey Pinkus to *The Guardian*. 'He could be in South America by now.'

After all, he had given himself two days to get away.

Besides, the sophisticated heist had none of the terror tactics of a daring robbery three weeks earlier when twelve men turned up on powerful motorbikes. Outside security guards wrestled with other members of the group who were trying to break security glass windows with sledgehammers. Three men were apprehended, even though they pulled firearms – one of which was a replica. They got nine years, but the rest of the gang escaped with £263,000 worth of diamonds, none of which has been recovered.

After these raids, security became much tighter. But six months before the latest heist, diamonds worth £200,000 were stolen by a charming 'new guy' working for a diamond certifying company.

'He worked for two years building up confidence and trust with people, then when somebody I knew gave him some diamonds to certify, he disappeared,' said Batcha Hussein, a local dealer in gold coins.

Hussein was one of those waiting to find out what had happened to the security box he rented for a couple of hundred pounds a year, after he had run out of space in his small safe. The contents, he said, were worth some £15,000.

'Some of the people will easily have lost half a million from what they had in there,' he noted. 'Most of us don't have insurance; we never thought we would be in this position. It's really shocking and upsetting for what went wrong. I'm anxiously waiting to find out what really happened.'

He was also shocked to discover that it was not as secure as he had been led to believe.

'We really thought it was the safest place in Hatton Garden,' he said. 'We only recently came to know that it's been robbed before.'

Within two days of the robbery being discovered, *The Sun*, under the headline 'Bag Blingo Blag Bigwig', was talking of the

'King of Diamonds' – the mastermind behind the heist, who the newspaper said had previously orchestrated the £40-million gems raid at a Graff store in London's New Bond Street in 2009.

On that occasion, two sharply dressed men arrived at the store in a taxi and entered, posing as customers. They made no attempt to hide their features as they had used a professional make-up artist to disguise them, using wigs, cosmetics and latex prosthetics (the make-up artist was told the two men were appearing in a music video).

As they were leaving the make-up studio, one looked in the mirror and said: 'My own mother wouldn't recognise me now.'

The other laughed and replied: 'That's got to be a good thing, hasn't it?'

The same studio had unwittingly helped disguise members of the gang that robbed the Securitas depot in 2006.

Once inside the Graff store, the two men pulled handguns. Shop assistant Petra Ehnar was forced at gunpoint to empty the store's display cabinets. The haul was 43 rings, bracelets, wristwatches and necklaces – one necklace alone was worth £3.5 million. Detectives investigating the robbery said later: 'They knew exactly what they were looking for and we suspect they already had a market for the jewels.'

Threatened with death, Petra was bundled out onto the street, where she was released. One of the gunmen then fired into the air to create confusion. The men escaped in a blue BMW, which was swapped for a silver Mercedes in nearby Dover Street. They switched cars again in Farm Street before disappearing, but along the way, they had rammed a black cab, and in their haste to get away, they had left a pay-as-you-go mobile phone wedged between the driver's seat and the handbrake. Numbers stored on the phone led police to the perpetrators.

JEWEL IN THE CROWN

In August 2010, after a three-month trial at Woolwich Crown Court, gang-leader Aman Kassaye was sentenced to twenty-three years in prison. Solomun Beyene of London, Clinton Mogg of Bournemouth, and Thomas Thomas of Kingston upon Thames each received sixteen years. None of the stolen jewellery was ever recovered.

Graff itself had its links to Hatton Garden. The 'King of Bling', billionaire Laurence Graff opened his first shop there in 1962 and went on to supply royalty and celebrities such as Donald Trump, Naomi Campbell and the Beckhams. The area had already come to the attention of thieves. In 1961, diamond dealer Meyer Van Moppes had his safe broken and 50,000 diamonds – then worth £175,000 – stolen after raiders drilled a hole through another building's wall. Then in 1972, notorious robber Bertie Smalls made off with jewels and cash worth an estimated £3.5 million today. Three years later, the Hatton Garden Safe Deposit Company lost an estimated £1.5 million in valuables through a raid.

The Sun's 'King of Diamonds' was also said to have been linked to a £13-million jewellery blag two years earlier, in 2007, on a Graff outlet in Sloane Street, when he and an accomplice turned up in a chauffeur-driven dark blue Bentley Continental. The thieves wore well-cut jackets and trousers, and posed as wealthy customers before pulling out silver handguns. After ordering the staff and customers to lie down on the floor, the men grabbed handfuls of rings, necklaces, pendants, earrings and diamonds, then walked out of the store to make their getaway.

An obscured image of one of the thieves – said to be black, in his late thirties and with connections to the Midlands – was caught on CCTV as he entered the store with his face partially obscured by a panama hat. The officer in charge of the inquiry,

THE GREAT DIAMOND HEIST

Detective Sergeant Sarah Staff, said: 'It is not every day that people use a Bentley to arrive at a premises they intend to rob.'

After the raid, the King of Diamonds moved to Spain, but was thought to have returned to England shortly before the Hatton Garden raid. It was clear that only a few villains could have been master draughtsman for such an audacious crime.

Retired Detective Chief Superintendent Barry Phillips said: 'There are less than a handful of villains left knocking about who could have acted as the draughtsman for this caper. It's inconceivable it could have been carried out without an inside man and that makes it more likely it was a British gang, rather than foreign, because Hatton Garden is such a tight community. You've got your major firms to the north, south and east of London who might be able to assemble the required expertise – and you cannot ignore the Graff fella.'

The Hatton Garden heist had the disguising marks of the villain who would use a Bentley, he thought.

'This was a very slick operation and the role of the draughtsman was vital to get the detail exactly right,' said Phillips. 'There simply aren't that many faces who could have done it.'

The planner behind the Easter crime caper, which was already being compared to the film *Ocean's Eleven* – would have scoured every inch of the building using plans and architects' drawings. Often the draughtsman was the brains behind a criminal outfit, a role made infamous by Bruce Reynolds, key planner in the Great Train Robbery of 1963.

Meanwhile, former Flying Squad commander John O'Connor suggested the diamonds would be laundered through the Russian Mafia.

'The De Beer diamonds targeted at the Dome were destined for the Russian Mafia,' he said. 'Russia is a diamond-producing country and it would not be difficult for the Russian Mafia to dispose of the diamonds taken.'

Gang members could end up with just 3 per cent of the value of their haul, he believed.

Diamond expert Fred Cuellar observed: 'They won't see anything like the reported headline figures because they can't sell their jewels through official channels.'

While the gang faced up to ten years' jail if caught, they would also be in danger from other villains as offers of big rewards flood the criminal underworld.

CHAPTER SIX

DIAMOND STREET

Two days after the theft was discovered, the police became more forthcoming. Outside the building, Flying Squad Detective Chief Inspector Paul Johnson announced that there were no signs of a forced entry.

'The thieves have disabled the communal lift on the second floor and then used the lift shaft to climb down into the basement,' he said. 'Once inside they forced open up to seventy safety deposit boxes. The scene is chaotic. The vault is covered in dust and debris, and the floor is strewn with discarded safety deposit boxes and power tools, including an angle grinder, concrete drills and crowbars.'

In fact, seventy had been opened, but five were empty and another eleven were due to be 'drilled out' due to non-payment of fees, leaving detectives to contact just fifty-six box holders. Other reports said there was jewellery all over the floor because the crooks could not carry it all, even though it transpired they made more than one trip.

THE GREAT DIAMOND HEIST

The thieves had used a £3,745 Hilti DD350 diamond-tipped coring drill to bore their way through a 50 cm- thick concrete wall into the vault, after bolting the drill to the wall to hold it steady. The drill weighed 77 pounds and was fitted with metal teeth (known as cores), which grind away at the surface to create a hole. It is capable of spinning at 667 rpm in top gear and needs a constant water supply to prevent it overheating.

Early estimates said that they could have spent up to 24 hours drilling through the wall, but it meant they were able to bypass the vault's 50-cm-thick metal door, which would have been more difficult to penetrate. Even to get to the vault itself, you had to pass through three other doors – one barred like a prison cell. If the guards at any point along the route don't recognise you, they won't let you pass. On 'Diamond Street' everything rests on reputation and the safe depository was thought to be impregnable.

'It's a sophisticated offence clearly and would take some pre-planning,' DCI Johnson said. 'The people who planned it knew how they were going to go about it. I imagine that pool of people is quite limited. Whether that involves some inside knowledge will form part of the investigation.'

Police were checking the status of current and former employees in the building, as well as people who had access. As the gang did not appear to have forced their way in, they assumed an insider must have helped.

The drilling alone took some specialist knowledge. Joel Vinsant, secretary of the Drilling and Sawing Association, said the gang must have had experience in using that type of heavy-duty drill, which is typically used to create holes for cables or ventilation systems, and requires a constant supply of water so that it does not overheat. It would have taken hours.

'They had to know the depth of the wall before they started out,' he explained. 'It would have likely been heavily reinforced with springs and they would have needed to bring the right drill bits. They may have bored several holes with a rig-based drill until they had space big enough to get through. It could have taken an hour per hole. If they weren't trained, they could have seriously injured themselves or got the drill jammed.'

Once through the wall, the gang would have used smaller drills and angle grinders to prise them open.

All this was of little comfort to the owners of the safe deposit boxes. By then just thirty of them had been identified and customers who had not been informed about the fate of their safe deposit boxes were growing restive.

Aadil Shaikh, an investment banker whose father had a deposit box with the company, said people were 'shell-shocked' and businesses had come to a standstill. People were angry as they still had not been told whose boxes had been affected.

'Either they have been broken into or not,' he said. 'We deserve an answer. It has been close to seventy-six hours and it is preposterous that we have been made to wait like this. Look around you, look at the industry, it is at a standstill. It is not a joke, people's livelihoods are at stake.'

Shaikh also believed it was a 'moot point' whether people were insured or not.

'If you insure a product, why on earth would you want to keep it in a safe deposit box? It defeats the purpose,' he said. 'We expect state-of-the-art security over here, this is Hatton Garden we are talking about, and this place had been broken into twice before.'

However, the gang had not been quite as clever as they assumed. They had thought that they had disabled the security cameras, but they were wrong. The *Daily Mirror* obtained CCTV footage showing them carrying off their huge haul in wheelie bins.

'This was clearly the work of a professional gang, who planned this job down to every last detail,' said a police spokesman. 'But they may have made a mistake in leaving this footage behind.'

The *Mirror* dubbed the six masked men shown: 'Mr Ginger', 'Mr Strong', 'Mr Montana', 'The Gent', 'The Tall Man' and 'The Old Man'. They had made two visits and the time signature allowed the newspaper to put together a rough timetable of events.

At 21.19 on Thursday, 2 April, staff at the safety deposit centre were shown locking up for the Easter weekend. Just four minutes later, Mr Ginger appeared. It was thought that he must have already been inside the building when the employees left. Wearing a blue jacket, dark trousers and latex gloves, he was carrying a large black sack over his shoulders. He kept his head down so his black flat cap hid his face from the camera but after a couple of seconds, he turned around, giving the camera a shot of his ginger hair. Turning again, he made his way downstairs towards the vault.

At 21.27 a CCTV camera in the street showed a white Ford Transit van pulling up at an alley beside the building; the alley was protected by a metal gate and the raiders would have needed a key to get through that. Police said there was no evidence of a forced entry. To reach the door, they would have also needed a further key to get past a metal gate that led from the rear alley on to the street. Men were seen pulling wheelie bins down the alley and then the white van drove away. It was followed closely by a dark Audi TT, although it had not been established whether this had anything to do with the raid.

The Gent arrived at 21.30. In the security camera inside the fire exit, he was seen wearing a balaclava under a hard hat and a high-vis jacket with 'Gas' emblazoned on the back. His dark trousers were tucked into stripy socks and he was seen to be wearing a smart pair of brown shoes and orange and cream gardening gloves. Carrying a large holdall, he too headed down to the vault.

Then Mr Strong turned up at 21.31. He was also wearing a hard hat and a hi-vis jacket, and was carrying a steel support. The Gent returned, wearing a dust mask. They moved tools into the building. More tools and holdalls were carried down towards the vault.

Five minutes later, Mr Montana appeared, so-called because his blue top had the word 'Montana' picked out in white letters. Two minutes after that, he and Mr Strong dragged in more wheelie bins. One was large and an air-conditioning pipe had to be moved out of the way to get it in. The gang then disabled the lift on the second floor of the communal office building and descended into the lift shaft to reach the basement, where the safety deposit boxes were kept in the company's vault.

The following morning, Mr Ginger was seen again at 1 a.m. Otherwise nothing more was seen of the gang above ground until they left the next day.

At 7.51 on Friday, 3 April, Mr Ginger, now wearing a baseball cap, balaclava and dust mask, brought two purple holdalls up from the vault. Mr Montana, now wearing a baseball cap and trainers, brought up two red tool boxes. It could be seen that the hair on the back of his head was closely cropped.

A minute later, The Gent brought up a monkey wrench and what was thought to be a large pair of bolt cutters, then he disappeared downstairs again. Ten minutes later, he reappeared with a large black bucket full of tools. Mr Montana and Mr Strong also brought tools upstairs and put them in a bag.

The three of them were seen chatting at the top of the stairs before a man with grey hair poking out beneath his hard hat appeared. This was The Old Man and he had had not been seen previously. They picked up the bags and went outside. The camera in the street caught them leaving at 8.12 a.m. A white transit van arrived outside. The gang loaded up their tools and drove off.

Nothing more was seen of the men until 22.17 on Saturday, 4 April, when Mr Ginger appeared, again wearing latex gloves and carrying a black sack. He went down to the vault. Then a new gang member – The Tall Man – appeared. He had a blue Nike bag over his shoulder and was carrying a red toolbox. No more activity was recorded until the following morning.

At 5.46 on Sunday, 5 April, The Tall Man re-appeared from the vault, wearing an Adidas tracksuit top and carrying two red toolboxes. He went down to the vault again, but quickly returned to get a tool. At 6.01, Mr Ginger, The Tall Man and The Old Man were seen at the fire exit. The Old Man and The Tall Man struggled to get a wheelie bin past the air-conditioning pipe again. Out of breath, The Old Man leant on the bin, giving the camera a clear shot of the side of his face.

There was more to-ing and fro-ing as the men took out bags and another wheelie bin. Outside the street camera caught a man arriving on a moped at 6.12. 'Moped Man' then walked down the alley, before making off at 6.37. Soon afterwards, the white transit arrived again. The robbers loaded everything on board and drove off.

The gang appeared to know the exact layout of the vault and even stole the CCTV system's hard drive to erase all footage of the raid – though not the secondary system that the *Mirror* gained access to. The newspaper had passed their copy on to the police, who again hinted that the thieves must have had inside help as there was no sign of forced entry to the building.

'What the gang have overcome to get into the vault is unbelievable,' observed Barry Phillips, who had once been Detective Inspector Johnson's boss. 'That takes a great degree of insider knowledge, expertise and ability to call on the experts who can breach the security arrangements. There are less than a handful of individuals who have the wherewithal to be able to get the insider information and the contacts and financial clout to put this job together.'

Phillips said there are three distinct phases to such elaborate raids: the planning, the execution and the rapid shifting of the most precious valuables abroad.

'The high-end jewellery will have already gone,' he said just a day after the investigation began. Nevertheless, he was confident that the culprits would be caught.

'No matter how sophisticated and well planned this raid was,' he added, 'no plan survives contact with the enemy. The villains give themselves away by their own stupidity and greed.'

The first phase of the investigation had officers sifting through intelligence records to establish which 'project' robbers were out on the street. These were the few criminal masterminds who have the ability to pull off the sort of outlandish heist that would have taxed the imagination of even a Hollywood scriptwriter. Again, it was said that the 'King of Diamonds' was the chief suspect. And investigators would be minutely picking over the crime scene.

'The forensic option is the best way of getting a successful conclusion,' said Nigel Mawer, former head of economic and specialist crime at Scotland Yard.

Clues from equipment left at the scene would also be a key

feature of the investigation. Detectives would be hoping that the gang had left DNA traces, fingerprints and even footprints in the dust and rubble created as they drilled through the reinforced concrete wall.

Another possible way of tracking down the perpetrators was 'turning' members of the gang for reward money. Mawer said some junior members might have been paid a fee, with only the bigger fish getting a share of the spoils.

'The bigger the job, the more it unravels,' he noted. 'The more people involved, the more prospect there is of people falling out, especially if big money is involved.'

Phillips recalled a drug gang that hid £1.4 million in assets in seven safety deposit boxes. One was so stuffed with £50 notes, Rolex watches and deeds to houses in Suffolk that it could barely be closed.

Another of the villains' weaknesses would an employee or former employee who provided the planners with details of the vault.

'Right now, police are looking for the inside man,' confirmed John O'Connor. 'They are also looking at the structure of the business and whether or not these boxes were insured.'

Phillips's officers had once been led to a cash-filled safety deposit box in the same Hatton Garden vault by one of the gang convicted in 1976 of robbing the Bank of America in Mayfair the year before. Thought to be the world's most lucrative bank raid of that the time, the gang got away with £8 million in cash, along with the contents of safe deposit boxes worth up to £22 million. Only £500,000 was recovered, though two of the convicted robbers – safe-cracker Leonard Wilde and used-car dealer Peter Colson – were served with criminal bankruptcy orders for £500,000 to prevent them using the proceeds. Wilde was sentenced to twenty-three years, while Colson received twenty-one years' imprisonment.

Others in the gang were sentenced to periods ranging from eighteen years for robbery to three years for receiving stolen goods. However, the man said to have masterminded the crime fled to Morocco, which has no extradition treaty with the UK.

Key evidence in the trial came from Stuart Buckley, an 'inside man' who turned police informant. He worked at the bank as an electrician and told officers the raid was the gang's second attempt. Previously, they had tried to drill through the lock of the bank's vault. But Buckley obtained the combination by hiding in the roof space above the vault door and peering through a hole in the ceiling as bank staff opened it.

After turning Queen's evidence, he was sentenced to seven years.

CHAPTER SEVEN

THE USUAL SUSPECTS

After a week, the police did not seem to be getting very far with their investigation, so *The Guardian* got on the crooks' trail. First on their list of suspects was George 'Taters' Chatham, who famously stole the Duke of Wellington's diamond-encrusted ceremonial sword from the Victoria and Albert Museum in 1948. He also once read in the press that one of his solo heists, carried out with a screwdriver and a piece of wire, was the work of 'an international crime gang'. However, Chatham had died in 1997, so had an unshakeable alibi.

Next, they were turned to former armed robber Jason Coghlan, who now advises people who have fallen foul of the law in Spain or Thailand.

'I would not be surprised if the men behind the raid were from Eastern Europe because that's where all of the best thieves come from these days,' he told the newspaper. 'I would be equally unsurprised to find out that the loot had very quickly found its way out of the United Kingdom and into Europe for disbursement to more friendly places to wash such hot gems and cash, which is very likely to be reinvested into the narcotics industry, because that provides a pension for villains to live comfortably off for life, rather than a potential headache hidden some place that it might be discovered.'

None of the loot was likely to resurface in Britain, he thought.

'People walking into a bank with a substantial amount of cash to deposit in the UK will find themselves answering questions from the police very shortly after filling out their deposit slip,' said Coghlan. 'Whereas taking bags full of cash into financial institutions in Thailand will manifest in being offered a comfortable seat and a cup of tea.'

Details of the Hatton Garden Heist gave another ex-armed robber from South London a frisson of nostalgia. It marked the return of the 'decent ordinary criminal' – not a terrorist, paedophile, rapist or psychopath who would beat his victim to a pulp on the slightest of pretexts.

'It's gone back to the old days, hasn't it?' he said. 'No one's been injured. No one's been shot. Everybody's happy because everybody's skint at the moment and they reckon – rightly or wrongly – that whoever's lost something can afford it.'

He did not know who had done it, though.

'Whoever it is has got very some good inside information about the alarm not working and they've obviously done their homework,' he observed. 'They knew the layout and they must have known that Hatton Garden is full of CCTV cameras so they'll have all been in disguise. Maybe they have military training but only certain people would have the balls – the audacity – to pull off something like that.'

What was clear to all concerned was that the haul was already on its way to foreign climes.

'This is no bunch of mugs,' said another former villain. 'They're never going to be nicking this stuff without it having a place to go to already arranged.'

Getting it out of the country would have been easy.

'It's a doddle,' he added. 'The same people who import drugs and weapons into Britain will be able to take anything out in the other direction. It won't be in a box in the back of a van, it'll be mixed up with something like a furniture assignment and I'd be surprised if it's not out of Britain already. And it will have all been split up, they won't have all their eggs in one basket.'

Chief executive of the Gemmological Association of Great Britain, James Riley, believed the watches, gold, diamonds, rubies, sapphires and emeralds in the safety deposit boxes were long gone.

'I am absolutely certain that these goods will not be disposed of in the UK,' he told the *Sunday Times*. 'The market is not big enough to swallow that quantity of illicit goods. Everybody is aware that the robbery has happened and will be on their guard.'

The jewels, he thought, were probably on their way to Antwerp, New York, Tel Aviv, Mumbai and Hong Kong.

Former London gang leader Corey Johnson said the heist had been carried out by top-level criminals.

'It's way above the street level,' he noted. 'The diamonds will have left the country within hours and they'll have agreed in advance where they were going to offload them.'

Old-fashioned bank robberies and break-ins had been on a long-term decline, thanks to improvements in security and the use of super-grasses. There were 847 in the UK in 1992, and just 108 in 2012. In London, the figures had fallen more dramatically – from 291 to 26 over the same period. Career criminals were taking to fraud and cybercrime, which hardly capture the imagination. Breaking into a high-security bank vault and rifling safe deposit boxes was much more dramatic.

The Guardian found clients of the Hatton Garden depository less forthcoming than the criminals. Most of the depositors who had darted anxiously in and out of the black door at numbers 88–90 in the days after the robbery refused to give their names, perhaps fearful of becoming a future target for thieves.

'People don't declare what they put in their boxes to stop this kind of thing from happening,' explained one jeweller. 'We don't want to be attacked. This is a dangerous business we're in.'

'The footballers and wealthy jewellers who had their goods insured will be OK,' noted another dealer, 'but these other characters will be the real ones to lose out. Their businesses will never recover.'

Established jewellers knew the dangers all too well and invested in their own extensive security systems, including state-of-the-art safes, CCTV systems and alarms.

'You don't want to be walking on the street with our goods,' said one. 'You're a marked man if you do that.'

But their clients often had no insurance because the contents of their boxes changed so frequently. For small traders, the consequences were disastrous.

'I'm fifty-six now,' said one. 'Imagine me trying to get a job after I've lost my entire livelihood. It's impossible; all the jobs go to the young people.'

Jeweller Micky Cohen said many small business owners had moved stock to the vault only recently after a local branch of HSBC announced it was closing its service.

'Most of us are in and out of there every day,' he explained. 'Most of the guys that have been affected will be ruined because they won't be insured. If it happened to me, I'd have to sell my house.'

Cohen also said the criminals would have targeted the smaller boxes containing individual diamonds as they are 'easier to offload'.

Other losses were more personal. One woman kept her late mother's jewellery in her deposit box.

'I couldn't afford to insure it, I couldn't afford to wear it – that's why I kept it there, I thought it was safe,' she explained. 'They were my mother's jewels, I had taken every precaution . . . I know a couple of people who kept their retirement plan down there. If people think it's only the rich who are hit by this, they are wrong.'

Séamus Fahy, the director of a similar vault in Dublin, said that clients were a mixed bag.

'You'll get ordinary people keeping a bit of cash, jewellery, the title deeds to their homes,' he explained. 'We do have clients who, if they are going out for dinner, will come to the facility and put on a necklace, and then come and bring it back the next day.'

This was because increasingly the wealthy feared aggravated burglary in their own homes.

'Thieves want rich people to be there when they break in,' Fahy added. 'They put on the kettle and tell their victims that before it boils, they want to know where the safe is. They are becoming more and more sophisticated, so if you have anything worth stealing, it's worth it.'

Fahy's Merrion Vaults in Eire are even more sophisticated than those in Hatton Garden. Here, clients use a personalised fob and code to pass through two doors before reaching reception, where staff behind bullet-proof glass identify clients as they give their biometric data to enter the vault.

'Even if you penetrated the outer wall, which you couldn't, there are laser beams, motion sensors,' said Fahy. 'If anyone tried to break in, an armed response would be on its way within minutes.'

The depository in Hatton Garden had no such facilities. It was an old-fashioned vault, which a skilled gang had found all too easy to breach.

Despite the seeming lack of progress by the police, there were still high hopes that the blaggers would be caught. Following the *Mirror*'s airing of the CCTV footage, its sister paper, the *Sunday People*, insisted that the police were closing in on the mob, quoting one insider as saying: 'When the gang saw the *Mirror*'s footage their hearts must have sank. They thought they had been so careful. This is their worst nightmare. They know someone will recognise them.'

Former Metropolitan Police detective Peter Bleksley said: 'It was an audacious crime – but now my money is on arrests and convictions. But I'm not so confident they'll recover the loot.'

The speculation was still that the diamonds had been swiped on the orders of some Mr Big and were now out of the country.

'It's only a matter of time before all the little details in the footage catch up with these guys,' said one Hatton Garden jewellery trader. 'One guy's hair. One guy's trainers. Somebody else's this, that and the other. The jackets – the gear is new. You've got six guys. They're all on CCTV. You've got a van, and a moped coming and going. Someone is going to talk and that person will talk to someone else. There were six of them in there but I can't imagine they are the only six to know. People blab.'

But Ex-Flying Squad boss Barry Phillips was now not so sure.

'There will have been sterile corridors so the junior members of the gang would not be able to inform on those higher up the hierarchical structure,' he said. 'The lower-level people will likely get caught due to greed and stupidity. They will be noticed in possession of a lot of money and someone will be willing to inform on them.'

He was confident painstaking forensic analysis would yield rewards, though.

'The amount of stuff they left behind has surprised me as that will lead back to individuals,' he added.

However, the police would have a tough time living down the fact that they did not respond to the alarm. 'It is potentially extremely embarrassing,' he conceded. 'If they had reacted, they could have walked into the villains doing the dirty deed.'

Although there was an enquiry into why the police did not respond to the burglar alarm, it seemed they rarely turned up.

'There's no real surprise there,' said a police source. 'The police have been degrading alarm calls for years. Unless suspects are seen, they are seldom attended and never at private addresses. The onus has been shifting towards owners. Blacklisting of businesses that have false alarms was common. Having said that, you would have thought that the owners would have taken a bit more interest themselves. The "bank holiday window" is, after all, as old as the hills.'

Security industry sources said that it was generally accepted that the police would not turn up to alarms unless the situation was extremely serious, such as posing a threat to life. Police forces were entitled to stop attending private businesses if they have more than three false alarms, and there had been speculation that the thieves had set off a series of alarms before the heist to ensure that officers did not show. However, the safe depository did not seem to be on the Met's blacklist.

The security guard who took only a cursory glance through

the windows was also being questioned by the police, but was not expected to take the blame. Others, it was thought, would feel the need to keep schtum, especially after the murder of Solly Nahome.

'There is a culture down here,' said a local jeweller who did not wish to be named for fear of reprisals. 'I know there are forces at work, I don't want to ruffle any feathers.'

He drew comparisons with a jewellery heist in 2004, where the perpetrators hid above his shop before breaking through a wall. They made off with a haul of £1.5 million and the raid had taken place over Christmas.

'It's so similar, it's untrue,' the shop owner said. 'It's exactly the same modus operandi. I reckon it's the same gang.'

Police sources said intelligence on the previous heist indicated that it was carried out by a gang of white men operating out of Bethnal Green in East London. They were never prosecuted. Some of the suspects were believed to match the description of the robbers caught on CCTV.

Meanwhile, DCI Johnson appealed to other businesses in Hatton Garden or members of the public who had CCTV footage or were witness to come forward. Building companies were asked to check if any of the gear seen in the footage, including a hydraulic jack and a nail gun, had gone missing from their premises. Some of the tools were of the distinctive red Hilti brand. The company had a trade centre in Southwark, less than a mile from the scene of the crime.

Of particular interest was the all-important drill. There were reports that it had been stolen from a shop on nearby Fetter Lane the previous December, but the serial numbers on the drill left behind had been filed off, making it hard to trace. Then Andrew Royce, boss of Elmcrest Diamond Drilling in Lewisham, South-

East London, came forward to say that equipment worth £80,000 had been stolen from his firm.

'We have the right sort of drills for digging into vaults,' he said. 'We've been offered jobs to convert old bank buildings into plush hotels and the like. The drills are all designed to cut through concrete or steel. They are all laced with diamonds. It would take a real pro to know what they are doing.'

A white Ford Transit van like the one used on the Hatton Garden heist was caught on CCTV stopping near the site around the time the equipment was stolen.

Another line of enquiry was a detailed analysis of the video. Detectives used face-recognition software and probed through files of known suspects to try to identify the culprits. Although the gang went to painstaking lengths to hide their appearance with hard hats, scarves and dust masks, some distinctive features remained visible.

Details gleaned from the video were also run by the Flying Squad's bank of underground informants and other sources within the criminal fraternity. They hoped that the pair of smart City-style shoes and striped socks worn by 'The Gent' might give them a name. Another key item was the hoodie bearing the word 'Montana' worn by another gang member.

The police said they were also trying to identify the number plate on a white Ford Transit used by the gang and seen for the first time on the recording. And they hoped the men might have stopped for food or something to drink at local cafés, including a McDonald's close by.

'The police incompetence has been staggering,' said Gerry Lander, whose box in the vault had not been opened. 'It is unbelievable that these pictures can be uncovered by the *Mirror*, while we heard nothing from the police.'

Former Flying Squad chief John O'Connor echoed those sentiments.

'I can't recall any major robbery or major crime where the media come along and get hold of the most convincing evidence that exists,' he said. 'They've obviously taken the view this is not high priority. They've got a graded response system and graded this very lowly. How could you possibly do that? I can't believe they can be so utterly incompetent.'

The Sun rubbed it in by warning that it was not the police the gang needed to look out for, but the Adams family, who were also after them. Tommy Adams lived near Hatton Garden in a £2.5 million house in Clerkenwell with his wife Androulla, while his brother and convicted armed robber Patsy – described by police as the A-Team's 'enforcer' – was said to have a major interest in a nearby strip club.

'The family are very well connected in Hatton Garden,' a source told *The Sun*. 'Traditionally, firms have been wary about doing any work there because of the Adams's reputation and the fact it is their "manor". The word is they had gear stored at the deposit centre and have lost a fortune. They are not happy.'

They need not have worried about Patsy, though. He had left the country with his wife shortly after the shooting of a man in Clerkenwell, in broad daylight, on 22 December 2013. The couple were arrested in Holland in August 2015 and extradited to face charges of attempted murder.

CHAPTER EIGHT

SPECIALIST KNOWLEDGE

When Mahendra Bavishi eventually spoke to the press, he expressed his fury at the police for ignoring an alert from the state-of-the-art alarm in the vault. The robbers had set off an intruder alarm just after midnight on Good Friday. This had alerted the Southern Monitoring Alarm Company, who contacted the Metropolitan Police's Central Communications Command. Police recorded the call, but graded it so that 'no police response was deemed to be required'.

'It is incredible that the police did not act on this,' said Bavishi. 'The police knew in advance that it would be closed over Easter so they must have realised nobody was meant to be in the vaults.'

There was no suspicion that Bavishi was in any way involved in the robbery. The police had not even contacted him.

'If they like, they can speak with me,' he told the *Daily Mail*. 'The police? Definitely, I will speak with them. Why not?'

Born in Sudan and of Indian heritage, he was a well-respected businessman and a former president of the Rotary Club of Khartoum. He ran the Manish Agency, which imports electrical goods to Sudan. His eldest son Manish usually managed the vault, but was away on a month-long holiday in the Sudan with his wife and child at the time. In his absence the business was being run by his younger brother, Alok.

'To many, this robbery is like something out of a Hollywood fiction film, but to my family, it is a tragedy,' he said. 'It is the end of the business my son has worked so hard to build slowly over the last seven years. It was making a loss when he bought it and only first made a profit last year, and even then it was very little. Before then we were relying on loans from banks as we worked to make it a success. Now the business is finished. Who will trust their valuables with us after this?'

Mahendra had been in China at the time of the break-in on unrelated business. He had returned to Khartoum, where Manish was making frantic plans to fly back to the UK.

'The police called Manish on his phone in Sudan to tell him what happened and said, "We want you to come back to London because there are sensitive issues we want to talk to you about",' Mahendra said. 'They told him they wanted to ask him questions that only he could answer about the business. The police want to know from Manish if he suspects someone inside, who could have contact with a gang. There must be suspicion on everyone who worked in that building.'

He admitted it was worrying that the thieves were so well informed.

'You know the way they entered is really surprising because if there is any vibration or even if somebody enters, if somebody tries to cut anything, all the sensors were fitted,' he added. 'I don't know how they got the information.'

SPECIALIST KNOWLEDGE

He said both the inside of the and the outer passageway were covered by CCTV and sensors and he was 'puzzled and surprised' at how they had managed to get past all the security measures. Meanwhile the police were re-examining an aggravated burglary in 2013 at Kenton, North London – the home of Manish Bavishi.

Rumours persisted that the Hatton Garden heist was an inside job.

'We were told that they went in five or ten minutes after the last member of staff came out,' said Peter Kirkham, a former DCI with the Met Police, who worked for the Flying Squad for five years. 'Not even a two-bit burglar would do something like that, let alone somebody attempting something like this. It stinks of an inside agent. And it's more their confidence that they would not be disturbed. I mean, I have never seen a job where they have taken a break, had a day off, and come back.'

However, he was confident that there would be plenty of DNA left at the scene.

'If I was investigating this case, I would expect my crime scene investigator to have found me something for the simple reason of how long they spent down there and the amount of surfaces they would have touched,' he said. 'With the best will in the world, it's very difficult not to leave something behind, especially nowadays we can use trace DNA.'

The other puzzle was why the thieves had only plundered seventy-two of the 999 boxes when they had so much time on their hands. By then the estimate of how long it would take to drill through the wall had come down to just 2 hours and 20 minutes to drill through the concrete wall into the vault, leaving the thieves plenty of time to rob boxes as they fancied.

'I'm not sure if they targeted specific boxes, or not,' said Kirkham. 'Or even if they went in for one thing in particular and took the rest because they were already there. But from what I understand, you have to drill through the boxes to get inside them and they would have had to use quite a heavy-duty drill. It has been suggested they may have just gone for boxes at waist-height because it would be easier for them to handle the drill at that height.'

Another former Flying Squad detective told *MailOnline*: 'Everything you see indicates a very specialist knowledge, both in what was inside the building and how to deal with it. There is an expertise, combined with strength, patience, determination and, probably, an inside knowledge.'

As there was no sign of forced entry to the outside of the building, this meant either that they had a key or that someone had let them in from the inside. The thieves also had detailed knowledge of the building. Having disabled the communal lift on the second floor, they used the lift shaft to climb down into the basement. From there, they had to break open shutter doors, before boring holes into the vault wall. Once inside, the gang wrenched open internal cage doors to get to the safety deposit boxes. These were prised open and emptied by the raiders, who left them strewn across the floor as they fled with their haul.

Former Flying Squad detective Jim Dickie was sure a professional gang had carried out the crime and it had been months, rather than weeks, in the planning.

'It's clear there must be an inside agent because of the level of preparation,' he explained. 'There's clearly an inside agent because of the preparation that's gone into it, including what sort of drills to use and being able to get into the building without disruption. The gang must have had plans to the vaults of the building and someone has allowed them in without forced entry. There is a clear expertise in the planning. As the pictures show, the thieves bypassed the vault locks and went straight through the wall, using a diamond drill bit.'

If the police were having little luck tracking down the thieves, the newspapers were hot on their trail. The *Mirror* called in former bank robber Noel 'Razor' Smith to analyse their CCTV footage. With fifty-eight convictions to his name, he had spent more than thirty years in jail, describing his criminal career as 'like an all-out war for me'.

Razor reckoned that a Mr Big had hired elite thieves from Eastern Europe and Israel to pull off the heist. They had been given a list of jewels to target. But the thieves got greedy and returned for a 'second dip' after no one reacted to the alarm going off. When no news of the raid broke on Good Friday or Easter Saturday, they returned for more loot.

'They took a huge risk, but they must have known it was worth it,' he added.

The perpetrator of more than 200 bank robberies before he turned his back on crime to become a successful author, Smith said: 'A Mr Big will have bought information from an insider, someone with a lot of knowledge about that firm, and assembled this crew. They will have been put up in luxury while they planned this, all with false identities, telling each other nothing about who they are or where they are from. It could have taken up to two years to plan something like this.'

He believed the stones would have been smuggled to Amsterdam, the diamond-cutting capital of the world. The thieves, though, did not have great technical skills – that was why the alarm had gone off. They knew about the CCTV camera, but it was too high up to disable.

'But what difference does it make if they can't be identified?' he said. 'They have hard hats, hi-vis jackets and masks. Every time they go past the camera it's heads down. They know the police have facial mapping technology, which is why they wear masks to cover their mouths.'

He thought that Mr Ginger was wearing a wig and the white van was either stolen, 'or more likely hired with false documents then dumped'.

Smith was surprised that The Gent had chosen to wear smart brown shoes for the blag while the others had worn trainers – after all, it was a reasonably athletic job. But again this did not matter.

'All clothes will be later burned in a furnace,' he explained. 'Anything connecting them to the scene will be incinerated.'

The use of wheelie bins, he thought, was inspired. They could carry a lot of stuff – including, presumably, the heavy Hilti drill – and people were used to seeing them. Smith said that they would have had lookouts with walkie-talkies outside. They would have watched out for any unusual activity after the alarm had gone off.

'Any police patrols or security guards would be reported immediately to the guys in the vault,' he explained. 'No news is good news.'

On the Friday morning, the thieves left, carrying equipment and holdalls. It was plain that they knew what they were doing – so far the job had gone with hardly a hitch. Then they got in the white van and drove off, free and clear.

'They will have laid low throughout Friday night up until Saturday night when they went back,' said Smith. 'During this period they'll be scanning 24-hour rolling news to see if their heist has been discovered. This is when I believe they got greedy and took a gamble. When no news broke, they decided to go back.'

SPECIALIST KNOWLEDGE

On the Saturday evening, Mr Ginger was seen back in the vault: it was a huge risk.

'He could be out the country by now spending the rest of his life a very rich man. Instead he's come back for more. I don't think this was part of the plan but criminals are greedy,' said Smith.

Mr Ginger, The Tall Man and The Old Man then moved another wheelie bin outside, which was probably full of gold, jewels or cash.

'The van they load up has a side door, perfect for that entrance,' Smith explained. 'The next half an hour is spent checking the place. Is there anything they have left behind that could incriminate them? They do a final sweep and leave at 06.44 in the white van. Job done.'

He believed that the gang had then left the UK to live on their ill-gotten gains, never to meet again.

'They have no attachments to each other or the job. On this evidence, the job was pretty watertight. In my opinion they'll disappear, never to be seen again,' Smith told the *Mirror*.

While others compared the robbery to various movies, criminologist Dr Richard Hoskins pointed out the uncanny similarity between the Hatton Garden heist and the plot of the novel *The Black Echo*, a thriller published in 1992 by the American author Michael Connelly.

'In *The Black Echo*, it's a long bank holiday weekend with the heist on the safety deposit boxes not discovered until the Tuesday morning when everyone returned to work,' said Dr Hoskins. 'Parallels right down to the alarm. It is so similar, it's extraordinary. It gets you thinking – did the thieves read the book?'

When contacted, Michael Connelly said: '*The Black Echo* was a fictionalised account of a bank heist that occurred in LA in September 1987. It was never solved.'

In the book, the heist takes place over the Labor Day weekend and the crooks use 'an industrial drill with a twenty-four-inch circle bit, probably diamond-tipped ... to cut a hole through the six-inch concrete wall of the stormwater tunnel'.

'As at Hatton Garden, *The Black Echo* burglars set off alarms constantly to confuse police, tunnelled through concrete over a long weekend and plundered safety deposit boxes,' said Hoskins. 'Smart thieves steal ideas from anywhere. The book was republished in the UK last year – did one of them read it? I think they probably did.'

As a rookie newspaper reporter, Connelly had written two unpublished novels set in Florida, before moving to LA in search of fresh inspiration and finding the 'Hole-in-the-Floor Gang'.

'I was doing a day in the life of the Los Angeles Police Department, sitting on the floor at a robbery-homicide division briefing about these guys, when I realised my book had dropped into my lap,' said Connelly.

The real-life raid had been on the First Interstate Bank at 7700 Sunset Boulevard in Los Angeles. At the time bank robberies were common in LA. There were about 2,000 a year in the 1980s, compared with 200 annually in the 2000s. But the First Interstate heist stood out.

'The Hole-in-the Floor Gang were exceptional – patient and skilled, like your Hatton Garden crew,' said Connelly.

In June 1986, the thieves had driven earth-moving equipment down the 12-foot-high storm drains that run under West Hollywood. They then took four weeks to dig a 100-foot tunnel.

'A few inches off anywhere and they could have missed the vault entirely,' Connelly explained.

The police estimated they removed 1,500 wheelbarrows of earth down their head-height tunnel. It was then carried out of the storm drains on all-terrain vehicles. The operation was timed so they had a long weekend to drill through the final three feet of concrete, undisturbed.

When the vault was opened after the holiday, staff found a neat hole 20 x 25 inches in the floor. Safe deposit boxes were strewn about and nearly $200,000 (£134,000) in cash and valuables was missing. The haul included a painting by the acclaimed French artist Henri Matisse.

The following year, the gang tunnelled into the Beverly Hills branch of the Bank of America and stole nearly $100,000 in cash. A third raid was abandoned after a city official inspecting the drains found the entrance to the tunnel under Wilshire Boulevard. According to Connelly, the gang were never caught and were last heard of operating in Buenos Aires.

Asked whether the Hatton Garden thieves had drawn inspiration from his book, Connelly said: 'It's all possible, I suppose. Crime is growing more global and skills are passed down between criminal generations.'

And he had another theory that connected the Hollywood and Hatton Garden raids. The gang members in both cases were skilled engineers, he thought, brought into the country by international crime bosses with the contacts and money to plan the job, then whisk the multinational crew out of the country when it was done. But the question remained whether the gangsters had read his books.

'We won't know for sure unless they are caught and admit it,' said Connelly. 'But why not? This is a specialist world and not many have the skills to carry off these heists. Cops may catch the robbers, but not the brains behind them.'

He also shared a sneaking respect for the thieves.

'There is no violence and they sweated for the money,' he added. 'And there is a certain class envy – we don't feel too sorry for people who keep fortunes hidden away in safety deposit boxes. Part of us hopes they are now lying on a beach somewhere.'

Seeking further literary precedents author Ben Macintyre drew a comparison between the Hatton Garden robbers and the real-life model for Sherlock Holmes's nemesis Professor James Moriarty – nineteenth-century master criminal Adam Worth. Under the name William Judson, Worth had rented a shop next to the Boylston National Bank, the largest bank in Boston, to sell 'Gray's Oriental Tonic'. Two hundred bottles of it were displayed in the window.

On Monday, 22 November 1869, the staff of the bank opened the vault to discover that it had been robbed over the weekend. The thieves had drilled through the wall from the basement of the shop into the bank. Neighbours had heard noises, but assumed it was building work. More than thirty tin trunks containing diamonds, jewellery, cash and securities had been prised open. The swag went back through the hole and out of the front door of the shop.

Under the alias Henry J. Raymond, Worth moved to Europe. From his large house on Clapham Common, he ran an international network of criminals. In 1881, he carried out a robbery in Hatton Garden, where an accomplice cut the gas main to extinguish the lights. Worth was able to escape with two sacks of uncut diamonds. Sir Robert Anderson, head of the Criminal Investigation Department at Scotland Yard at the time, described him as 'The Napoleon of Crime' – a sobriquet that Arthur Conan Doyle applied to his character Moriarty in the short story 'The Final Problem', first published in 1893.

SPECIALIST KNOWLEDGE

The audacity of the Hatton Garden heist may well have inspired others. Barely ten days later came news of a similarly audacious piece of jewel robbery in North London. Taking his cue from the movie *Mission Impossible*, a masked burglar scaled the two-storey wall of an antiques market in Hampstead, broke through a two-foot roof-top vent, squeezed down a flue, picked three sets of locks, then crawled his way along a floor to avoid infra-red security beams to steal 124 watches worth some £200,000 in total. The haul included an 18-carat gold Goliath 8-Day Swedish royal presentation wedding pocket watch from 1910 worth £12,500 and an 18-carat gold Verge Fusee watch made by Thomas Earnshaw of London worth £9,000. The owner of Hampstead Antique and Craft Emporium said the whole raid took less than eight minutes in total.

'It was very much a *Mission Impossible* thing,' he declared. 'He managed to squeeze through a vent that is two-feet high and wide. He clearly knew what he was doing and was methodical. It was probably the tidiest burglary in history, he cleaned up the counters and made sure everything was clear.'

Despite dodging many of the surveillance cameras, much of the theft was filmed by a camera in the ceiling. Nicknamed 'The Snake', the burglar was wearing a dark hooded jacket, jeans and Nike trainers. He escaped by shimmying back up the ventilation shaft and into a waiting 4x4. Returning with an accomplice the next evening, the pair fled when neighbours heard noises and called the police. A balaclava, screwdriver and ladder were found at the scene.

The Hatton Garden thieves may also have drawn inspiration from a gang in Germany, who drilled through 80 centimetres of reinforced concrete to enter the vault of the Volksbank in Steglitz, south-west Berlin, in January 2013, after spending weeks digging a 100-foot tunnel from a lock-up garage rented under a false name. When the bank closed on Friday afternoon, they drilled four massive holes through the walls of the underground vault, then opened 294 safe deposit boxes, stealing diamonds, gold and silver valued at more than 10 million (£8.3 million). The Berlin bank was still negotiating with more than 100 of the box owners, who did not have theft insurance.

The Volksbank mob were thought to have come from Eastern Europe as the wooden boards used to construct the tunnel came from Poland, and bottles of Polish beer were left behind, along with a Polish translation of *American Desperado*, the autobiography of drug smuggler Jon Roberts. Again, an inside man was suspected. German police obtained DNA samples of some of the gang from the scene of the crime and released video footage and artist's impressions of the thieves, but had been unable to trace them. There was speculation that the same gang could be responsible for the Hatton Garden heist. In both cases, gang members posed as builders.

When pictures were released of the three connecting holes drilled through the wall in Hatton Garden – measuring 25 by 45 centimetres – they looked almost identical to the four connecting holes in the wall of the Berlin bank.

Comparing the holes, a drilling specialist said: 'You can't operate this gear without having a good deal of training. Whoever made that hole has done it a good few times before. You can see the wall is reinforced with steel and it would have taken an expert to get through it.'

Former flying squad detective Jim Dickie said he was in little doubt that Scotland Yard detectives would be liaising with their German counterparts about the Berlin raid as a legitimate line of enquiry.

'The modus operandi is very similar and there will only be a number of criminal gangs who have the audacity and the knowledge to carry out these sorts of crime,' he told *MailOnline*. 'There is the high level of planning; the drills used – even the drill bits – and the fact that they have got into the building without disruption, probably with the help of an inside agent. Both have had a very sophisticated level of planning.'

The power tools used, including the heavy-duty Hilti DD350 drill, were the same as those found at the Berlin heist.

After pictures of the hole in the wall of the Hatton Garden vault were released, the *Daily Express* speculated that the gang had employed a contortionist on the raid. The hole was just 10 inches high, 18 inches across and 20 inches deep (roughly 25 by 45 by 50 cm). This led the paper to suggest that the thieves had borrowed a tactic from the movie *Ocean's Eleven*. A five-foot Chinese acrobat called 'The Amazing Yen' – played by Shaobo Qin – played the 'grease man' in the raid in the 2001 film starring George Clooney and Brad Pitt. In 2004, the Beijing contortionist reprised in the role in *Ocean's Twelve*. Contortionists or not, the thieves who ransacked the Hatton Garden vault certainly had to be of a slim build.

Meanwhile, the first inklings came that the Hatton Garden heist might itself be made into a movie. Former fiancé of tragic singer Amy Winehouse Reg Traviss was at work on the script. The cockney film director's latest movie *Anti-Social* had just premiered.

'The heist got me excited, a hundred per cent,' he said.

CHAPTER NINE

THE PLOD

The Metropolitan Police looked even more bungling when an office worker stumbled upon more CCTV footage a week after the crime had been discovered. Taken just 50 feet from the crime scene, it was said to contain 'crystal clear' high-definition images, much better than the footage the *Mirror* had discovered. The employee had dialled the 101 non-emergency number because she assumed detectives already had similar footage, but police scrambled to her workplace to seize the tape.

'It is unreal it took this employee to bring these images to the attention of the police,' said a local trader. 'The footage could be crucial in collaring the crooks. You would assume the investigating officers had done everything they could to get CCTV footage. In my opinion it just reinforces the idea this serious crime is not being investigated as seriously as we would hope. People are baffled – we're talking about tens of millions of pounds and hard-working people being left out of pocket.'

THE GREAT DIAMOND HEIST

A spokesman for Scotland Yard would only say: 'The Metropolitan Police has obtained and is examining a substantial amount of CCTV footage in relation to the burglary at Hatton Garden Safe Deposit. This footage has come from many different places. We will not discuss the specifics of the CCTV we are examining and will release information in a timely manner for appeal purposes only. Police continue to seize CCTV with assistance from members of the public as the investigation progresses.'

Perhaps stung by the criticism, the Met sent in a seven-strong specialist team for a 'deep search' of the premises, looking for evidence behind panels, under floorboards and in other hidden areas. They were seen carrying out two large plastic bags. One was marked 'clinical waste'. The other, marked 'MP', was clear plastic and was seen to contain Costa coffee cups, mineral water and cola bottles, and packaging from a Clairol Nice & Easy hair dye kit. The team had recovered some 400 exhibits, including items for DNA profiling, fingerprints and other evidence. Specialist forensic photographers also snapped the crime scene and used digital techniques to record 3D images of the inside of the premises.

Detective Superintendent Craig Turner, head of the Flying Squad, said: 'The hours of forensic work and inquiries have been vital in order to ensure we are able to exploit all investigative opportunities to their fullest extent and assist us in identifying those individuals responsible. We appreciate that this situation has been frustrating for those affected by this crime and thank those individuals for their ongoing patience and support. Those safety deposit boxes not opened by the thieves during the burglary have been left secured as they were found throughout the examination. HGSD are in the process of making contact with owners to arrange collection ... Of the seventy-two boxes opened during the burglary, we have only been unable to make contact with six people who we believe have been a victim of crime. We continue to make efforts to trace them.'

At a meeting at the London Diamond Bourse, victims of the robbery were told that they were unlike to get any of what had been stolen back. Harry Levy, president of the LDB, said: 'I was very pessimistic when I spoke to the people who have lost everything. I said that the possibilities of recovering money are very limited. You never recover money from these big robberies.' Many of them were uninsured and claimed to have lost their livelihoods.

'Some will find they have lost a roof over their heads and won't be able to trade any more,' he added. 'They are lost souls.' He advised them to form a committee and consider employing a lawyer and loss assessor.

Mirza Baig, a jewellery dealer, told ITN News: 'I don't have a penny's worth of stones left with me because they were all in the safe deposit – the safest place you can imagine.'

Loss adjuster Rick Marchant told of dealers who were 'sobbing, devastated' when they learnt that it was unlikely that their goods would be recovered. He was dealing with seven clients who had lost items worth up to £2 million. These included a dealer who had lost diamonds worth £1.3 million and a pawnbroker in his late fifties who had placed jewellery, watches, silverware and pens in his deposit box. They were items he had taken in exchange for about £20,000 in loans, meaning he could not recover the cash. Tragically, he was diagnosed with cancer a few days later and could not work to recover his losses.

'I have been told by individuals I have interviewed that they have had friends and colleagues who work in the quarter with them, grown men, hardened dealers, in sobs – [they] don't know what to do because of course some haven't insured at all,' Mr Marchant told the BBC. 'These aren't extremely wealthy people, for a lot of them their livelihoods have gone. All of us might be forgiven for thinking how audacious, how clever, but what they've done is ruin the lives of many people within the Hatton Garden jewellery quarter.'

Other dealers claimed they had been left in the dark. The police had said that valuables, including gold bars too heavy to carry, had been left strewn around the floor of the vault.

Another insurance adjuster said: 'All the victims have given statements but some have been invited back to look at what police found on the floor of the vault. Those meetings haven't happened yet. It could hold up insurance claims so they want them to hurry up. One of my clients said that the police told him there were only half a dozen items found, another said hundreds, so the picture is unclear. The traders are pretty peeved, particularly those that are uninsured. They need to be really transparent about this.'

A gold dealer in his sixties told how he lost gold and other precious items worth hundreds of thousands of pounds when his box was looted. He was from India and said: 'We lost everything in Partition and now we lost everything again in London.'

To him, the raid was a mystery.

'There are several theories,' he explained. 'I mean, why so few boxes raided? Maybe they were looking for something in particular.'

His daughter said that they had been expecting to speak with detectives about whether they owned any of the discarded items. But those talks had not taken place.

Clearly this was not a victimless crime. In an appeal for

witnesses on the BBC's *Crimewatch* programme on 23 April, a paltry £20,000 reward was offered for information leading to the arrest and conviction of the gang responsible. Detective Superintendent Craig Turner also appealed to those close to anyone who knew how to use a heavy-duty drill: 'We are keen to hear from wives or partners of anyone who has specialist knowledge or skills that use this sort of equipment. Were they away during the Easter bank holiday weekend or have they been acting oddly since the burglary was carried out?'

Meanwhile, drilling experts had been at work again, this time at Britain's oldest wine merchant, Berry Bros. & Rudd, established in 1698. The company opened its flagship store on St James's Street, London, in the seventeenth century. Its customers include the poet Lord Byron and William Pitt the Younger, Britain's youngest-ever prime minister, and they had been vintners to the royal family for over a century.

Thieves had cut a hole in the wall of one of their warehouses in Basingstoke, Hampshire, and made off with bottles worth more than £100,000. While the Hatton Garden raid had taken days, the Berry Bros. thieves were in and out within 30 minutes.

'There was a large hole in the warehouse wall and the wine taken was of high value, with one case worth over £5,000,' said a spokesman for Hampshire Police. 'It is believed a six-figure sum was taken from the warehouse but the exact figure remains unknown at the moment. It looks as though a van has been used because of the amount of wine taken.'

With the Flying Squad seemingly mired, after just three weeks the BBC jumped in with two feet and aired *Britain's Biggest Diamond Heist? The Inside Story.* This might be considered premature as the police would not allow presenter Declan

Lawn and his camera crew into the building. However, a man who worked in the building allowed them in the side entrance that the robbers had used. But to demonstrate what the thieves were up against, the show resorted to library footage showing the opening of the Hatton Garden Safe Deposit over sixty years earlier. The voice-over with the black-and-white clip stated: 'Constructed at a cost of over £20,000 a two-foot-wide bomb- and burglary-proof door opens up a labyrinth of safes.'

That £20,000 would be the equivalent of £500,000 now.

Lawn explained: 'Many of the diamond dealers in this area are small businesses and relied on this safe deposit company to store their precious stones. It failed them. Some are not insured and are frightened to speak out.'

However, he found one dealer who would speak to him anonymously. In a local café, with his back to the camera and his voice heavily distorted, the dealer said that he knew people who had been devastated by the loss of both their livelihood and any pension they had been accumulating. They were in a terrible state.

It was not just that they were financially ruined, he added, 'It's more than that, it's what you've done your whole life that's been taken away from you.'

On the BBC's website, Lawn explained that he tried to follow in the footsteps of the thieves to show what it would take to pull off the biggest diamond heist in British history. First, he went on a reconnaissance mission to Hatton Garden with former British Army surveillance operative Chris Regan. His task was to try and pick up as much information at he could from the streets around the depository building to assess its security, as the burglars had.

In Hatton Garden, he tried to blend in with the crowd, but found it remarkably difficult. The private security guards soon spotted him and he found himself under constant surveillance from CCTV cameras.

'You stand out because you look like you're up to no good,' Regan told him. 'You feel guilty, and you look it.'

He thought the gang would have devised some obviously innocent reason for being on the street, perhaps conducting a survey or handing out leaflets. Regan reckoned, if he was planning the heist, he would put in several months either getting a job on the street or renting an office in the target building. It was a job that you could not pull off with intelligence gleaned by opportunistic street surveillance, but by exact information from people on the inside. Even on the night of the raid, there would have been surveillance on the street to give warnings about security guards.

One of the ways to get the information needed was to rent an office or a room overlooking the building some months before, Regan added. Then all you would have to do was look out of the window. If he were the police, he would be getting the rental records of every office in the depository building and every building surrounding it.

Even then, it was still unclear how the burglars had got into the building. The speculation was that some inside the building simply waited for the last person to leave. Otherwise they could have gained access, clambering over the adjoining rooftops.

'One day last week – while the police investigation unfolded downstairs – I managed to talk my way into the access laneway at the side of the building, the very place where the thieves were captured on CCTV,' said Lawn. 'If I could manage blagging access in ten minutes' flat, imagine what an organised gang could do over several months.'

In the documentary, Lawn turned to one-time career-criminal-turned-journalist and author Noel 'Razor' Smith. He told the presenter: 'I think if you are going to put a job like this together properly then what you will do is the typical *Reservoir Dogs* turnout, where you will get people who don't know each other and therefore if one falls, all can't fall.'

But this proved not to be the case.

'How do you know the person you are bringing in isn't going to talk to the police?' asked Lawn.

'The criminal . . . sort of underworld if you like, for want of a better word, works on reputation,' said Smith. 'And if your reputation has even got a stain on it, nobody will talk to you.'

The BBC used the CCTV footage showing one of the robbers entering the building at 9.23 p.m. on 2 April, carrying a large black sack and keeping his head down, obscuring his face from the camera. Seven minutes later, they were seen bringing in the tools they needed to pull off the job.

'The first challenge is how to get to the vault, which is located in the basement of the building,' said Lawn. 'There's a security door on the ground floor, which prevents access to the stairs leading down to the vault. But the robbers have crucial information about the workings of this building. They know that there is a lift shaft that goes all the way to the basement. But as part of the security of the vault the lift itself does not go down that far. The gang has worked out that if they can climb down the lift shaft, they can bypass the security preventing access to the basement. To do that, they first have to disable the lift.'

To do this, he consulted lift engineer Gary Kennedy, who produced a key that looked like a socket wrench. When inserted in a small key hole above the lift door and turned, it allowed the door to open when the lift was not there, giving the robbers access to the lift shaft. It also broke mechanical and electrical contact, disabling the lift, preventing the cage from moving and allowing the outer door to be opened onto the empty shaft when the cage was not there.

Kennedy had disabled the lift when the cage was above the door, as the thieves must have done. Despite admitting his twin phobias of heights and confined spaces, Lawn was given a quick course in abseiling by two expert mountaineers. He then attempted to abseil down a lift shaft as the thieves had done. This was a complicated business using cables, clips and harnesses. Suspended on a rope attached to the bottom of the lift and swinging around in the dark, this was no easy task, even though Lawn was relatively young and fit.

'Up to six robbers came down the lift shaft this way with all their tools,' he explained to viewers.

Next, they would have had to clamber up around a metre and a half and spring the lift door from a catch at the top. Although he was assured by Kennedy that he was in no danger, the cage above him in the narrow still looked ominous.

'Don't forget the basement door to the vault was probably bolted or screwed shut,' said Lawn. 'So you probably had to have cutting equipment in the shaft with them. Police photos show how the robbers then forced open this security door from inside the lift shaft and then cut the bars on the last door leading to the vault. So they had made it this far. They were in the basement corridor outside the vault, just one step away from the boxes. On the streets above, no one was aware that one of the world's biggest heists was unfolding.'

At twenty past midnight, three hours into the heist, the robbers tripped an alarm. The company monitoring the alarms called the police, but they decided that they did not need to respond.

'Alarms aren't that much of a deterrent,' Smith explained. 'We used to do a place where the alarms were going and nobody would turn up. You know you've got a certain amount of time to get out. So if the alarms went off, they may even have set off the alarm on purpose, just to see what the response was.'

But since Smith quit his criminal career, alarms had become a great deal more sophisticated. Lawn admitted that it was difficult to tell how the thieves had disabled the alarms at the Hatton Garden Safe Deposit without being allowed into the building.

Showing more CCTV footage, he said: 'It's nearly one o'clock in the morning. The gang are so confident that they haven't been rumbled by the alarm going off that one of them is seen on CCTV around half an hour later and then disappears for the next seven hours to the basement, where they are dealing with the next big obstacle, drilling through the outer wall of the vault.'

Next came crime-scene photos released that week, showing how the gang got through the wall.

Lawn and his crew then set out to discover just how difficult it was to drill through reinforced concrete, so he consulted a drilling specialist named Greg Marrison, who set up a block of reinforced concrete the same thickness as the wall of the vault with the drill attached to it.

'We've got the same drill, making an identical hole, and a team of six, just like the robbers,' said Lawn.

Then Marrison set the drill running against the clock. It proved surprisingly quiet.

'Everyone has been asking how on earth residents and security guards didn't hear loud subterranean drilling,' said Lawn. 'But when you're operating a drill, it becomes clear why more people weren't disturbed. It's diamond-tipped and it doesn't vibrate like a drill you might have at home. As it slices inexorably into the wall at the exertion of even a little pressure, it emits a steady whine that isn't anywhere near as loud as you expect. You can talk to the person beside you by just slightly raising your voice.'

However, even a diamond-tipped drill should have generated enough vibration to trigger a sensitive alarm.

The diamond bit cut quickly through the concrete, but each time it hit the steel reinforcement, it slowed down dramatically; the first hole took 1 hour 13 minutes to drill. The other two holes alongside it were much quicker to cut and to make a breach the same size as that made by the robbers took just 2 hours and 19 minutes – much quicker than earlier estimates.

'This was like a military operation,' said Lawn.

He reckoned the thieves could have been in the vault by about 2.30 p.m. on the first night, but there was a problem: Lawn discovered that he was too big to fit through the hole. Although he managed to get his head and one arm through, his shoulders were too broad. However, a slim young man from the production team managed to get through in his place.

'When you look at the CCTV, at least two or three of those guys are bigger, sturdier guys, my size or even bigger,' noted Lawn. 'So they did not all go into the vault. So the police should be looking on the CCTV for the ones who are leaner, thinner – they're the ones who were in the vault.'

The documentary then turned to former Flying Squad detective John Jones, who had investigated some of Britain's biggest robberies. He was surprisingly chipper about the theft.

'It was the sort of classic heist,' he observed. 'Highly well planned, loads of cheek, presumably great profits, and it really took me back to the old days when professional criminals used to do these kind of things rather than what they tend to do these days, which is sell large quantities of dangerous drugs.'

For balance, the BBC then turned to former South London

gangster Dave Courtney, who lived in a semi-detached 'castle' surrounded by British flags in Plumstead, South-East London, close to where he grew up. Patriotic to a fault, Courtney wanted to crush the idea that the heist was pulled off by a foreign gang.

'I can understand people going, "Oh yes, very KGBish, very Eastern Bloc military trained, you know, like *Mission Impossible*,"' he said. 'There's not many criminals think it's a Russian firm.'

Indeed the criminal fraternity were convinced that an English team was responsible. It was 'incredibly ballsy and audacious,' said Lawn.

'That's what that sort of criminal is about,' Courtney told Lawn. 'He's incredibly ballsy and gutsy and risky, and me and you ain't prepared to do that and there are some people who would. That's the difference between them and you, my friend.'

Different members of a team bring different skills. According to Courtney, you did not necessarily have to get clever people: 'If you have enough money, you can buy the skills, you can more or less Google it.' After all, as he pointed out, you can hire mercenaries to go and fight a war in a foreign company, if you have the cash. Such things were available on the 'dark web'.

Meanwhile, Smith had another view.

'The team that went in there were labourers,' he explained. 'Basically, they done the heavy work, they do the donkeywork. There's someone above them and puts the team together. They could be on a flat fee.'

This could cause difficulties in such a lucrative heist.

'The problem with that is, if you are on a flat fee, once you see how much you have stolen, some people get a bit bitter and twisted, and that could lead to their downfall,' he observed. 'I would say they were probably on a percentage. I would always work it that way when I was working. Even the driver got a percentage and that way nobody's bitter because they are all getting a share.'

To complete the heist experience, Lawn attempted to open a safe deposit box. He had no prior experience of this, he pointed out. First, he tried with a hammer and chisel. After some thumping, he managed to detach the outer casing. Then he attempted to knock the lock into the box. Finally, the door flew open and he pulled out the metal container inside.

The first box took him roughly five minutes to open so then he took a sledgehammer and pounded the door of a second one. After three swings, the door fell off. It had taken less than forty seconds.

'All of this is significant for the investigation that is now ongoing, because it gives a very different perspective on the timeline of the raid, and even the real motivation of the thieves,' explained Lawn. 'In short, my experience suggests they had more than enough time to open far more boxes than they did. In fact, even if they had only been in the building for only one night, and only one man had gone into the vault, they could easily have opened more boxes.'

From the police photographs, it seemed that the doors on the safe deposit boxes remained on their hinges, suggesting they had opened them by drilling the locks out, which would have been even quicker.

'So why not just open every box in the place?' he asked.

'After working for nearly eleven hours through the night, the robbers leave the building at 8.05 a.m.,' Lawn continued. 'For the next two days, the robbery scene lies undiscovered. Incredibly, the gang then returns on Saturday night to plunder more safe deposit boxes.'

Was Smith surprised that the thieves had gone back for second helpings?

'Not at all, it's typical of criminals,' he declared. 'I've done it myself. If you go past a job the next day and you're watching the news and there's nothing about it on the news, and when you pass by and it all looks the same as the way you left it, you're going to take a chance to go back in. It's too tempting.'

This seemed to fulfil the old adage of villains always returning to the scene of the crime and Smith insisted that he had returned for more plunder on several occasions.

'If it's still cool, you go back in to see what you can get,' he added.

What was still puzzling was, when the thieves left the building for the last time at 6.30 a.m. on Easter Sunday, after all their hard work they had only opened seventy-two of the 999 boxes.

'Why not go for more?' mused Lawn. 'After all, other boxes could have contained jewels worth millions.'

Courtney believed they might have known which seventy-two of the boxes to target. Indeed, he thought there may have only been one box they were after. This again pointed to the heist being an inside job.

'Obviously, there was some kind of inside help, however trivial,' he said. 'One hundred million per cent, someone had to help them somewhere with it. Without a doubt.'

'When you consider the value of some of the diamonds stolen, that theory starts to gain credibility,' agreed Lawn. He had met a Hatton Garden diamond dealer who said he lost over 200 jewels in the heist, with a total value of nearly half a million pounds. The dealer had lost a pair of diamonds that together were worth £40,000 and one four-carat diamond worth £60,000. While he did not wish to be identified on camera, he showed

Lawn certificates of authenticity for some of the stones that he supposed were now out on the black market.

The dealer also said that, until just a few days before this robbery, he was holding a diamond in his deposit box that was worth £300,000. But he took it out just in time. He said he believed that the reason why so few boxes were opened was because the diamond thieves had intelligence from the international diamond market about which dealers in Hatton Garden had the most expensive stones and they went for those boxes. But this was just one of many theories floating around Hatton Garden at the time.

Another thing Lawn found puzzling was that the owners of the safe deposit company had not been in contact with those who had had their safe deposit boxes rifled.

'We haven't heard anything and we think that is actually making it look bad for them,' said a dealer. 'Obviously they should be here supporting us and supporting their business.'

Lawn said he had tried time and again to make contact with Manish Bavishi.

'I just want to ask him about why he has not been in touch with the customers we've spoken to,' he explained. 'He's been running the company for the last eight years. I tried calling him. Whoever answers claims not to be him and says they don't know where he is. I tried contacting him on social media and called on an address where we were told he stayed.'

He had also spoken to people who said Manish was abroad, and he had spoken to people abroad, who said he was in the UK.

'Have you any idea where he is?' Lawn asked a dealer.

'I've not heard of him being around,' the man said. 'You would expect that he would come back.'

Lawn found this odd.

'I think "disappointed" is more the word,' the dealer wryly added.

Having failed to get in touch with Manish Bavishi, the BBC arranged a telephone interview with his father, Mahendra Bavishi, in Khartoum. Mahendra said that he had last spoken to his son before he left for London just a few days after the robbery.

'Do you find it odd that you have not been able to contact him since?' asked Lawn.

'Well, I know the situation he is in and I'm sure after he finishes with all this hassle, he will call me,' Mahendra replied.

Lawn then raised the possibility that the robbery was an inside job and that somebody working there was implicated.

'Well, I don't think so,' said Mahendra. 'I don't know how they got the information, but I don't think that could be the case.'

He added that people had not been in touch with him about the heist, although you might imagine that detectives would want to speak to everyone involved in the case. Again, he insisted that he was perfectly willing to speak to the police if they contacted him.

The final part of the jigsaw the BBC looked into was what could have happened to the loot and Lawn directed this question to Smith.

'You take it to a slaughter, where it will be chopped up and parcelled,' Smith said, explaining that 'slaughter' was a criminal expression for a place where thieves cut up jewellery into unidentifiable pieces.

'The loot will be broken down into small parcels and given to people who probably won't know what's in it, just be paid a fee to go onto ferries,' he added.

Lawn asked whether giving people bags of jewels wasn't a bit risky.

'They don't even count people out of the country, let alone check anybody,' Smith observed.

Courtney had a far more intriguing solution to the problem of smuggling large amounts of stolen jewellery out of the country: it was to buy a racehorse and stick a bag of jewels up its backside.

'People have done that?' asked Lawn, puzzled.

'Millions of people have done that,' said Courtney.

'People have put jewels up a horse's bum to get them out of the country?'

'Very much so – hundreds and hundreds.'

Lawn then asked Courtney whether he thought the thieves would get away with it.

'I think they have got a very, very, very hard job,' said Courtney. 'The amount of money that is going to be offered to be an informant . . .'

'So if the reward is big enough, there'll be someone in the underworld who will . . .?'

'One hundred per cent.'

Ex-detective John Jones did not think that they would get away with it.

'Someone always talks,' he said. 'Other criminals get jealous. They know what somebody's done and they haven't got any, so they will tell their friend, who will tell a police officer.'

But if they did get away with it, Lawn concluded, they would have got close to pulling off the perfect crime.

As the documentary went on air, none of the thieves had been caught and most suppositions about them later proved incorrect. However, Lawn found one beneficiary of the crime that he could interview on camera – a local locksmith. Since the heist, his 'phone had been ringing off the hook', he said. On one of the jobs he had picked up, he had been paid in diamonds – in the shape of a pair of diamond earrings that he was going to give to his daughter for her birthday.

He had renamed them 'The Heist'.

CHAPTER TEN

NABBED

Six weeks after the heist had been discovered, the empty speculation shuddered to a halt when seven men were arrested in connection with the robbery. They were not Polish 'plumbers', Serbian ex-servicemen or engineers from Argentina: they were British bulldogs – and proud of it.

On the morning of 18 May 2015, more than 200 officers raided twelve addresses in London and Kent. Four suspects, aged forty-eight, fifty-eight, sixty-seven and seventy-four, were arrested in Enfield. A fifty-year-old man was detained in East London, while a man aged seventy-six was held in Dartford, along with a fifty-year-old. They were described as white British males and 'proper old-guard London gangsters'. Later, another two men, aged forty-three and fifty-eight, were arrested. What was surprising was that they were all comparatively old; three of them were pensioners. The gang which, until then, had been known as the 'Diamond Geezers' were now being called the

'Diamond Old Geezers', although the *Daily Express* preferred to dub them 'Dad's Army', while the *Sun* began referring to the heist as a 'pension fund raid' and called the culprits 'Diamond Wheezers'. Even the *Financial Times* joined in the fun, calling them 'silver safecrackers'.

Commander Peter Spindler, head of the specialist crime command at the Met, was quick to raise a hurrah for the men of the Flying Squad.

'At times we've been portrayed as if we have acted like the Keystone Kops but I want to reassure you that, in the finest traditions of Scotland Yard, these detectives have done their utmost to bring justice to the victims of this callous crime,' he declared. 'They've worked tirelessly and relentlessly, they've put their lives on hold over the last six or seven weeks to make sure that justice is served.'

Spindler again defended the Met over their failure to turn out when the alarm had gone off.

'On this occasion the systems and processes that we have in place with the alarm companies weren't followed,' he conceded. 'And as a result of that officers did not attend the premises when in fact they probably should have done; and for that, I want to apologise. However, the keyholders were notified about alarm activation and the security officer was sent to the premises. That security officer saw what our officers would have seen had they deployed, which was a multi-occupancy building on eight floors, where in fact the premises would have appeared secure and no alarm was sounding. We have an ongoing review into the defeat of the alarm. We're going to work very closely with the alarm industry to make sure that this doesn't happen again.'

The police announced that they had recovered several large bags at one house containing a 'significant amount of high-value property' – said to be gems, gold, jewellery and other valuables. Detectives were confident the items recovered during the searches had been stolen in the burglary, but Detective Superintendent Craig Turner, head of the Flying Squad, urged victims of the crime to 'stay patient'.

'Police officers will be in contact with them in order that we can restore this property back to its rightful owners,' he explained. 'Please be patient in relation to this.'

The alleged gang members had been under 24-hour covert surveillance for up to a week after detectives received intelligence suggesting they were involved in the raid, he added. Armed officers had been on standby during the arrests but did not enter any of the properties targeted by police. They were still appealing for information about a white van, registration number DU53 VNG, which had been seen in the area at the time of the raid. Meanwhile, officers were keeping guard outside a house in Enfield.

The police released pictures of the van seen in the Hatton Garden over Easter. DS Turner appealed for more information about it.

'It was a white Transit van, registration DU53 VNG, which was caught on CCTV near Hatton Garden Safe Deposit Ltd,' he said. 'We have had the CCTV from an early stage of the investigation but we are now releasing the registration of the van. Did you see anyone loading or unloading a white van in the Hatton Garden area over the Easter bank holiday? So far we haven't managed to recover the van yet. Have you seen a van matching this description and registration since the burglary in Hatton Garden, or do you know where it is now?'

Among those arrested were seventy-six-year-old car dealer Brian Reader and his fifty-year-old son Brian, known as Paul.

THE GREAT DIAMOND HEIST

They were picked up at their detached home in Dartford Road, Dartford, Kent, at 10.30 a.m. and taken to a London police station for questioning. The pair ran a second-hand car dealership called Pentire Cars from their £800,000 Dartford home. Their website promised 'fantastic savings' and 'competitive prices'. One local described the father and son as 'filthy rich'. Their five-bedroom house, hidden behind high walls and trees, was protected by a state-of-the-art security lighting system and burglar alarm.

The arrest was witnessed by neighbour Kevin Watson.

'It was just after ten o'clock. About three vans full of police turned up. There were maybe twenty or more officers,' he said. Some were in full riot gear, others were in plain clothes; they came in from three directions.

'They surrounded the property, entered and shouted "Police, police!"' he added. 'It was quite orderly and peaceful. There was no fight. Then, about half an hour later, they brought the younger man out, handcuffed, and put him in one of the vans. Fifteen minutes later, they brought out the older guy, who seemed to be struggling a bit health-wise. He was holding his chest. They took the younger one back in momentarily, which was to get medication presumably. He came out with a bag.'

The older man was also seen to be uncomfortable, holding his stomach.

Delivery driver Jon Donadio was also a witness to the arrest.

'I was in my van and I pulled up on the side of the road,' he recalled. 'I saw the police with riot gear and I thought it was unusual. I saw the police, quite a few of them, all in blue police suits with peak caps. They had an old guy – he was in his mid-sixties or seventies. I parked up to do a delivery outside the drycleaner's. I saw them bring him out in handcuffs. He was being led out, there was no struggle; he came quietly.

They tried to make it look low-profile by draping something over the handcuffs.'

According to Watson, the officers stayed for about an hour, then forensics arrived and remained in the property all day. Another neighbour said that the family had recently been carrying out building work.

'They were always building and working on their houses, so it was horrible to have to live so close to them,' she said. 'There would be constant banging, all day and night.'

Over the objections of the neighbour, the Readers had been building two new homes on the site.

'I didn't know him socially,' she added. 'He has been living here for a while. We haven't seen him for several weeks, since Easter. He keeps a very low profile.'

Silvia Castelao, whose home backs onto the property, said that she had heard the two men having a stand-up row two days before they were arrested.

'They were shouting and swearing at each other really loudly,' she recalled. 'I could not believe it because they are supposed to be father and son. But whatever the argument was about they were going crazy with each other – with lots of swearing and shouting.'

She had already had trouble with the pair.

'When they first started the building process, they started building and burning things really violently, so violently that bits of ash were coming over to our property,' she explained. 'They were not being considerate and the ash destroyed my daughter's trampoline. My husband went over to speak to them and they said it wasn't their problem.'

The police cordoned off the private road leading to the Readers' house and carried out extensive searches of the grounds and outbuildings on the plot. Dressed in forensic suits and white masks, officers used pitchforks and shovels in the garden and looked through bushes. They were also seen using a metal detector on a patio area.

Forty-eight-year-old Irish plumber Hugh Doyle, a Dubliner, was another of those being questioned. He was arrested at his £600,000 semi-detached home in Riverside Gardens, Enfield, North London. A female neighbour said: 'He was a really friendly and helpful chap, the type of guy you could rely on. It's left us shocked and unsettled.' He was also described as 'hardworking' and 'a family man', and said to be a Manchester City supporter and an action-movie enthusiast.

It was thought that the married father-of-two had given up a job in the City to retrain as a plumber and he ran a business called Associated Response. A high-powered motorbike bearing the firm's livery was parked outside his house in Riverside Gardens. A Facebook page linked to the company showed Doyle piloting a variety of small aircraft and crewing a yacht with friends.

Sonia Crouch, who lives opposite Doyle, described how a coach-load of police officers arrived in their quiet street at 10 a.m.

'I was looking out my window and I saw a van outside,' she said. 'At first I thought it was an ambulance, but then I put my glasses on and saw it was a police van. All of a sudden all these police in really black clothes all marched out and down the end of the road.'

Her husband John added: 'You could see they were there with the Flying Squad because there were about three plainclothes cars and a police car. The coach was all blacked out. My brother used to live three doors away from him. He said he was quite a nice bloke.'

Another neighbour said: 'We had him here in the house to

do a plumbing job up in the loft. But it wasn't very well done. The water started coming through. He said somebody else would come but nobody came. That was a bit disappointing. He was friendly – over-friendly. I am more shocked than anything else. He had so much work to do, with his vans always coming and going.'

An elderly neighbour who lived a few doors away expressed her shock at the police raid, saying nothing like that had happened during her forty-six years of living in the street.

'They were there when I came to open the gate to the dustman at 8.30 this morning,' she recalled. 'Everyone knows him. The local pub knows him very well. He was not a bad man – he was a helpful person, always willing to lend a hand. I am just very surprised. He has two lovely kids and I am so sorry for his wife. It's terrible when I see that people are such nice people, and then you come across these sorts of things.'

The police were left guarding the house after Doyle's partner Jenny and their two young children departed. A forensics team then moved in and paid particular attention to his bedroom.

Other houses in Enfield were subsequently raided by the police and sealed off. At one in Park Avenue, owned by fifty-eight-year-old Daniel Jones, a Mercedes was taken away for forensic examination.

Another of those arrested was sixty-seven-year-old former shopkeeper and property dealer Terry Perkins, who was living in a Victorian terraced house in Heene Road, Enfield, less than half a mile from Doyle in North London. Police visited three Enfield addresses linked to the Perkins family. Those were the homes of Perkins's daughters, Vicky, Terri and Laura, none of whom were arrested. The police also searched the Enfield home of a woman in her fifties named Valerie Hart.

A team of police were seen removing a number of items from the house and impounded a black Land Rover Discovery. A neighbour said: 'Police turned up at around 10 a.m. yesterday and they have been coming and going ever since. I've seen them searching the back garden and I also saw police taking away a black jeep.'

A neighbour reported seeing two men being led from the house: 'I heard all the noise and came out and saw two men being taken away in handcuffs. That must have been at about half eleven. They were both elderly gentlemen.'

Another witness to the raid said there was a loud commotion when two transit vans full of police officers swooped on the property.

'The police were running up and down the street at about 10.15 a.m.,' she recalled. 'There were two massive vans going up the road. They tried to gain entry through one of the houses adjacent. One of the policemen had a ramming thing . . . some were wearing helmets with visors. There were quite a lot of people going in with those forensic suits.'

One of those in custody was said to be the architect of the raid, who had been arrested after a tip-off from an underworld supergrass. A source told the *Daily Mirror*: 'The suspected mastermind is regarded by those who know him as a brilliant mind and a great strategist. He was arrested using intelligence from an inside man.'

Following the raid, detectives searching a detached bungalow in Enfield, North London, were seen removing a dozen evidence bags, including one containing a box for a Hilti drill.

Harry Levy, president of the London Diamond Bourse, praised the police on behalf of the dealers whose livelihoods had been threatened.

'They were very canny,' he remarked. 'They kept a low profile as far as the recovery is concerned and they came up trumps.'

He told BBC Radio 4's *Today* programme: 'I've been quite sceptical about recovery of any property. I was absolutely delighted when I heard yesterday that they had recovered quite a substantial amount of, as they put it, "high-value property". We have absolutely no idea what they have recovered, but I am sure this will come out quite shortly. At least there is light at the end of the tunnel now as far as people are concerned in recovering their property. But I think it's going to be quite a long process of, (a), sorting out the goods and, (b), finding out what belongs to what.'

However, not all the victims were pleased that stolen property had been recovered. A relative of one of those affected told the BBC they were 'probably worse off' after the police raids: 'With the stolen goods vanished, there was pressure on insurance companies to settle quickly to enable holders to trade again. Now, with a whole mess of stuff to sort out, it may drag on for months. If batches of the stones were mixed up, it may be impossible to reunite them with their owners.'

Certainly, there would be problems. The *Daily Mirror* was told: 'We are talking about thousands of diamonds and other jewels mixed up together and some of it was already stolen when it was stolen. There is no inventory of what was in the vault and not all the owners of the boxes have come forward, so working out who owns what will be a huge headache. Some will undoubtedly remain unclaimed.'

But as the police shifted through the valuables they had seized and reported that they had recovered 'all or very nearly all' the gems and jewellery taken, Harry Levy became more cheerful.

'We were all delighted with the wonderful news the police

released regarding the arrests and recovery of a substantial amount of high-value articles,' he told the *Daily Telegraph*. 'Many of us were surprised. Some of us thought the police would eventually make some arrests but did not think they would recover any property. Many were initially frustrated that they were unable to enter the vaults to remove goods from boxes which had not been opened. About two weeks after the discovery of the robbery, a small group from the London Diamond Bourse met the police. They explained the vault was a crime scene, goods had been scattered over the floor and they had to collect and collate these goods, as well as obtaining forensic evidence. When we heard the news yesterday, we immediately emailed Detective Superintendent Craig Turner, whom we had met in the Bourse, and congratulated him and his team on their wonderful achievement. I was one of the sceptical members from the trade but I'm glad I've been proved wrong. As regards to the recovered goods, those who were uninsured are, of course, happy to know all or some of their goods should now be returned to them. The London Diamond Bourse will continue to work with the Metropolitan Police to give guidance on which agencies can assist with identifying the property they have recovered with the objective of returning the items to the owners as quickly and smoothly as possible.'

But jewellers in Hatton Garden were still disbelieving.

'I cannot believe they didn't get it all out of the country,' said one. 'My boss was laughing – he thought they must have been sitting on piles of the stuff. Everyone had thought it must have been an inside job. They should have had cutters ready to go, make it all look different, get it on the black market. Once it's out of the country, it's gone.'

Knightsbridge jeweller Michael Miller said: 'The police said they retrieved large bags of high-value items, I don't know how they can relate that to the actual burglary. The last thing I heard was the police were asking people who had their boxes broken into to come in and identify their property, so it might take a couple of days or weeks.'

Daniel Caspi, a local jeweller, welcomed the news of the arrests.

'If the goods that have been recovered are those from the Hatton Garden theft, our only concern is that they be returned as soon as possible so the jewellers concerned can carry on with their livelihood, which has been put on hold for the past few weeks,' he said. 'The next stage . . . the goods are returned speedily to their rightful owners. The main concern is the efficiency at which this will be handled, that the goods won't be held back from them to stop them from working, for evidence or any prosecution that may happen in due course, and be bogged down in the legal system for two or three years. That's our only concern.'

Doyle, Jones and Perkins, along with fifty-nine-year-old William Lincoln of Winkley Street, Bethnal Green, and seventy-four-year-old John Collins, a twenty-year resident of Blestoe Walk on an Islington council estate, were all charged on 20 May with conspiracy to burgle. The Readers and fifty-eight-year-old Carl Wood of Elderbeck Close, Cheshunt, Hertfordshire, faced the same charges. All eight were remanded in custody to appear before Westminster Magistrates' Court on 21 May. A ninth man was bailed pending further enquires, while a tenth, a forty-two-year-old from Essex, had been arrested and was being questioned at a London police station.

CHAPTER ELEVEN

OLD-TIMERS

What struck everyone was how old the men who had been arrested were. The *Financial Times* asked how had such a vintage contingent managed to abseil down a lift shaft? How did they manoeuvre such a large drill into position? And how on earth would Michael Caine, Ray Winstone and Bill Nighy divvy up these characters when the inevitable film is made? A *Guardian* reader proposed that Brian Cox, Martin and Gary Kemp, Vinnie Jones and Shane Richie also be considered for parts, while the *Daily Express* applauded the return of 'proper British crime'.

'Let's face it, crime simply hasn't been the same since the arrival of Romanian gangs, Chinese cyber crooks and Somali warlords,' the *Express* noted. 'We miss the days when crims spoke English, loved their mums, believed in honour among thieves, had names like Fingers or Shortie and could all be played by Ray Winstone in a movie. And not only are the Hatton Garden suspects homegrown, they are also oldies. Like the rest of us, career criminals must work until they drop.'

Other newspapers pointed out while this bunch of apparently harmless seniors had been nicked, bankers who had swindled billions out of the public walked free. There were no dawn raids on their palatial establishments.

When the defendants appeared in court, they were described as 'grey' or 'balding' – and one of them appeared to be deaf. They had a combined age of about 490. Seventy-four-year-old, grey-haired John Collins struggled to hear what was being said and needed to be helped by co-defendant Paul Reader, whose seventy-six-year-old father wore a comfy-looking brown cardie. They arrived at court in a convoy of police vans and unmarked cars. Despite their advanced years, they were accompanied by armed guards, while police helicopters circled overhead and armed response vehicles waited in the sealed-off streets outside the court. After a jangle of keys, the accused limped and shuffled into the glass-fronted dock and stood in two rows as the charges were read out.

'Wearing cardigans, tracksuits and jeans, they looked more like a group of friends on a golfing holiday and spoke only to confirm their names and addresses,' said the *Daily Mirror*.

Some even had reading glasses slung around their necks. Supporters packed the public gallery. Some waved at the men in the dock. By then *The Sun* had christened them the 'Over-the-Hill Mob'. *The Times* said it looked 'like a casting call for *Last of the Summer Wine*'.

Addressed by the clerk of the court, Collins appeared puzzled.

'What she say?' he asked in a thick East London accent. 'I can't hear.'

'Do you have an address? Somewhere where you live?' the clerk repeated slowly.

Unemployed fifty-nine-year-old ex-mechanic and lorry-driver William Lincoln also struggled to hear what the clerk was saying. He gave his address as Bethnal Green, where he lived with one of his three daughters.

Prosecutor Edmund Hall told District Judge Tan Ikram: 'This is a notorious case, which has been the subject of much media attention. Some seventy-three safe deposit boxes were opened. The full value has yet to be ascertained but it runs to in excess of £10 million.'

He said the men were arrested following a 'lengthy and detailed' police investigation, codenamed 'Operation Spire'. A quantity of the stolen loot had been recovered, but detectives were still searching for missing jewels.

Putting the charges to the men, the clerk said: 'Between April 1st and May 19 you conspired with each other to enter or trespass a building in Hatton Garden, namely the Hatton Safe Deposit Company, with intent to steal.'

There were no bail applications and all eight were remanded in custody to appear at Southwark Crown Court on 4 June. The judge warned: 'The allegation is a serious one, which would carry a lengthy custodial sentence if convicted.'

Conspiracy to burgle carried a maximum jail term of ten years, but sentencing guidelines recommend between one and five years.

The day after their appearance, a ninth man, forty-two-year-old taxi driver Jon Harbinson of Beresford Gardens, Benfleet, Essex, was also charged with conspiracy to burgle in connection with the Hatton Garden heist. He had held a Hackney Carriage licence for the past twelve years and usually worked in the afternoons and evenings around the eastern side of London, including the City and Liverpool Street Station, not far from Hatton Garden.

The father-of-three told detectives: 'I am totally innocent of any involvement in this burglary in Hatton Garden. I am not a thief. I have worked hard all my life. I presently work six days a week as a taxi driver to provide for my family.'

He claimed the first he knew of any family member being involved in the burglary was on the previous morning when his aunt told him that his uncle, the defendant William Lincoln, had been arrested for the high-profile burglary.

'I am totally innocent about this matter in Hatton Garden,' insisted Harbinson. 'I am unable to help police in this matter in any way. I have morals and I would not nick anything.'

Nevertheless, when Harbinson appeared before District Judge Quentin Purdy at Westminster Magistrates' Court, wearing a dark blue sweatshirt and grey jogging bottoms, he was remanded in custody to appear at Southwark Crown Court on 4 June with the other defendants.

On 4 June, the nine men made their appearance by videolink from Belmarsh high-security prison in Woolwich, South-East London. When officials struggled with a patchy connection, Terry Perkins suggested that it would be easier to meet face-to-face.

'Ask the judge and yourselves to come down to Belmarsh and we can have tea together?' he said, provoking laughter in the courtroom.

Another joked about 'being on telly' as prison officers and court officials tried to ensure everyone could hear. In a broad London accent, defendant Daniel Jones told the woman clerk: 'Tell your mate with the bald head to stop talking!'

The less-than-hirsute male usher appeared upset by the remark.

With staff attempting to correct the problems with the

videolink, the suspects could be heard complaining, with one calling the situation 'a farce' and 'a joke', another adding: 'This is s***!'

The problems were not over once the hearing began, though. Judge Alistair McCreath was interrupted mid-flow with an automated message saying: 'Your conference will end in two minutes.'

The exasperated judge pressed on – only for the videolink to be cut with the message: 'Your conference is now over.'

'Oh, for heaven's sake!' he sighed.

He remanded the men in custody until September, with the trial date being set for 16 November. Later, four more people were charged with concealing criminal property and were bailed to appear in Woolwich Crown Court on 4 September. Meanwhile, the Hatton Garden Safe Deposit Company closed down, due to a slump in business after the raid. The premises were put up for sale.

Despite the fault with the videolink, the *Financial Times* was warning that the proceedings were far from a joke. The Hatton Garden heist, followed by a robbery in Cannes, days before the Film Festival, where masked thieves made off with 17.5 million in watches and jewellery at gunpoint, had created a spike in the insurance market. London was the world's biggest insurance market and the rates were shooting up.

The following week, *The Sun* reported that it had found the 'Blingo Blag HQ' – the hideaway where the robbers had planned the heist. It was a single-storey warehouse in the grounds of a pub on a quiet suburban street in North London. The brick building, with its black wooden shutters and doors, was rented by a plumbing company around eighteen months earlier, but they hadn't moved in until October 2014. In the months leading up to the raid, neighbours heard drilling. CCTV footage saw a group of men leaving shortly before the premises were raided by plainclothes officers six weeks after the robbery.

Other officers were looking into the possibility that the murder of ageing gangland figure John 'Goldfinger' Palmer was connected to the Hatton Garden heist. Until his death, the sixty-five-year-old was under surveillance by a team based for security reasons in an unlisted office in RAF Spadeadam, on the borders of Cumbria and Northumberland, as it was alleged that he was protected by high-ranking Metropolitan Police officers in his pay. The Spanish authorities also bugged his home on Tenerife.

Palmer earned his nickname for his involvement in the Brink's-Mat robbery. While he was found not guilty of robbery, he admitted melting down the gold bars from the heist in his garden, but claimed he did not know they were stolen. In 2001, he was jailed for masterminding one of the largest timeshare frauds on record. When he went away, he was thought to be worth £300 million. Released four years later, he was declared bankrupt, with debts of £3.9 million. It seems that the Adams family took over some of his assets.

He was arrested again in 2007 for running his criminal empire from his British prison; also fraud, money laundering and possession of an Uzi. His fortunes seemed to have revived a little. He was living in an isolated cottage on the edge of Weald Country Park near Brentwood, Essex, though he still kept his palatial eight-berth yacht in Tenerife.

When his body was discovered, the police and paramedics who were called to the scene mistook the shotgun blast to his torso for a scar from recent gallbladder surgery. Post-mortem examination revealed that the shotgun had been loaded with

Right: CCTV images dated 2 April 2015 showing, from top, the raiders arriving in the Hatton Garden Safe Deposit building; (centre) the elusive 'Basil', the only member of the gang still at large; and (bottom) the white van used by the gang outside the building before the robbery.

Upper: 'The thieves had used a £3,745 Hilti DD350 diamond-tipped coring drill to bore their way through a 50 cm-thick concrete wall into the vault.' Safe-deposit boxes can be seen in the background.

Lower: The scene inside the vault, showing the smashed-open boxes.

Above: Getting careless – police surveillance shots of John Collins (above left) and Brian Reader (above right) at Scotti's Café, Clerkenwell Green, on 17 April 2015, after the raid.

Both © Metropolitan Police/PA Wire/Press Association Images

Centre: Hugh Doyle (left) and John Collins caught on CCTV at the rear of the Old Wheatsheaf pub, near Doyle's workshop, in Enfield on 18 May 2015.

© Metropolitan Police/PA Wire/ Press Association Images

Bottom: Left to right: John Collins, Terry Perkins and Brian Reader in the Castle pub in Pentonville Road on 1 May 2015, from a police surveillance video.

© Metropolitan Police/PA Wire/ Press Association Images

Left: Detective Chief Inspector Paul Johnson of the Met's Flying Squad reads out a statement at a press conference outside the Hatton Garden Safe Deposit building on the morning the raid was discovered.

© *Yui Mok/PA Archive/Press Association Images*

Centre: Brian Reader, the oldest of the robbers, who was sentenced to six years and three months in jail. According to his lawyer, and given serious problems with his health, he is likely to die in prison.

© *Metropolitan Police/PA Wire/Press Association Images*

Below: Top row, left to right: John Collins, sentenced to seven years, Daniel Jones (seven years), Terry Perkins (seven years); bottom row, left to right: Carl Wood (six years), William Lincoln (six years), Hugh Doyle (twenty-one months, suspended for two years).

© *Metropolitan Police/PA Wire/Press Association Images*

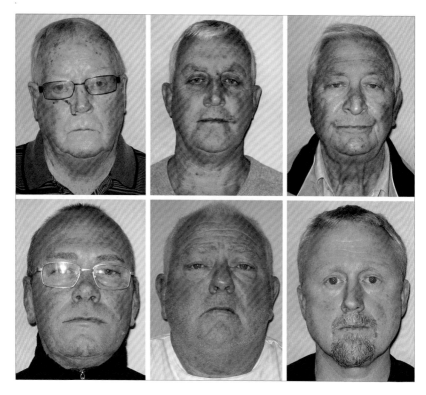

ammunition containing lethal wires, designed to shred the internal organs. He had been shot several times. There was little doubt that it was professional hit. A man was later arrested, but released without charge.

On 4 September, the three oldest members of the 'Dad's Army' gang – Brian Reader, John Collins and Terry Perkins– along with fifty-eight-year-old Daniel Jones, admitted their role in plotting the heist. They also faced a charge of conspiracy to convert or transfer criminal property. But the prosecutor Philip Evans QC said the Crown would not be pursuing the charge in light of their guilty pleas to the more serious offence.

Three others – William Lincoln, Hugh Doyle and Jon Harbinson – denied conspiracy to burgle and launder the proceeds, while Reader's son Paul and Carl Wood had yet to enter pleas. When they appeared in court on 30 September, they too denied conspiracy to burgle and to transfer stolen goods. On 9 November, Paul Reader was released from Belmarsh after all the charges against him were dropped. His sister Joanne and other relatives were waiting to greet him as he left the prison and his solicitor, Hesham Puri, said: 'We're relieved the CPS has seen sense.'

His father remained inside, awaiting sentencing, though. Apart from sight and hearing problems, he was suffering from prostate cancer – on 30 January 2016, he was taken to hospital in an ambulance with an armed guard for treatment for cancer It – and he also had a stroke while in prison; he also needed assistance to carry out simple tasks.

Meanwhile the police were still looking for the stolen goods. At a pre-trial hearing at Woolwich Crown Court, Philip Evans QC said: 'It's fair to say the amount which has been recovered is very significantly less than the amount taken. The process of identifying those figures is long and complex but the Crown states a significant amount of jewellery is outstanding.'

At that time over £5 million was still thought to be missing, though estimates were soon revised upwards. Danny Jones complained that so much was still missing because the police had ignored his offer to show them where his share of the £20-million haul was stashed.

In a letter to Sky TV journalist Martin Brunt from his cell in Belmarsh, Jones wrote:

> I've instructed my solicitor to tell the Flying Squad that I want to give back my share. They said it's in motion. I now understand that the police said that the prison won't release me to the police. What a load of bull. The police can't want it back as I'm the only person in the world to know where it is, deep down. I want to do the right thing and give it back. They are trying to make me look a bad person. I'm trying my best to put things right.
>
> If I don't get the chance to go out under armed escort, I hope some poor sod who's having it hard out there with his or her family find the lot and have a nice life. You'd have thought the police would have jumped with joy. But for some reason which I don't know, they are not that interested.

He could not understand why the authorities had not accepted his offer.

'They took that sex killer Levi Belfour [Bellfield],' he said. 'He showed the police where he killed those women. So, there you go . . . a sex killer and there's me, a fifty-eight-year-old burnt-out burglar. Maybe they think I'm going to get a hit squad to get me out. My God, how stupid!'

Responding to the allegations, a Scotland Yard spokesman said: 'We are not prepared to discuss an ongoing investigation.'

In a second letter, three weeks later, Jones wrote:

> I haven't heard. They better hurry up. We don't want anyone finding it, do we? Knowing I'm going to prison for a long time all I want to do is let my two sons no [know] I'm trying to change for the best. I no [know] I've done wrong. I'm not crying, Martin, I did it. I can't talk for other people, only for myself and whatever I get on judgment day, I will stand tall, but I want to make amends to all my loved ones and show I'm trying to change. I no [know] it seems a bit late in my life, but I'm trying...

Eventually, on 15 October, Jones was allowed out under armed guard. He took detectives to Edmonton Cemetery in North London to show them where he had buried his share of the loot while a police helicopter circled overhead. Following this, he was then immediately taken back to jail while a team of a dozen officers in forensic suits began excavating, while ten more stood guard.

The following day, a spokesperson for the police said: 'Met flying squad officers searched a venue in North London as part of an ongoing investigation, where property was recovered.'

'It's staggering, but he delivered,' a source told *The Sun*.

Jones insisted that he had revealed the whereabouts of his share of the haul because he wanted to 'make amends'.

'I've done wrong,' he told Sky News. 'I can't talk for other people, only for myself, and whatever I get on Judgement Day, I will stand tall, but I want to make amends to all my loved ones and show I'm trying to change.'

The old lag, it seemed briefly, wanted to mend his ways.

CHAPTER TWELVE

THE CROWN VERSUS...

On 16 November, Carl Wood, William Lincoln and Jon Harbinson appeared in Court Two of Woolwich Crown Court in South-East London, charged with conspiracy to commit burglary between 17 May 2014 and 5 April 2015. Hugh Doyle also appeared. He was jointly charged with them on one count of conspiracy to conceal, convert or transfer criminal property between 1 January and 19 May. They all denied the charges and spoke only to confirm their identities.

Doyle turned up in his black work clothes, carrying the logo of his plumbing company, having been out on bail. The other three had been in custody. Dressed in a long-sleeved light blue polo T-shirt and sporting a faint moustache, Lincoln again asked for the clerk to speak up. At sixty, he was the oldest of the four defendants. His white hair was receding and he wore glasses.

Harbinson was also balding and he wore a plain white shirt. Wood wore a beige cardigan and sported a brown beard, greying at the chin. Both he and Lincoln wore headphones in the dock to follow the court proceedings.

The jury comprised six men and six women, with two additional women being sworn in as spare jurors. Before they were empanelled, Judge Christopher Kinch QC, the Honorary Recorder of Greenwich, asked: 'Do you have any close personal connection with the jewellery trade in general, or the Hatton Garden area in particular, or with any person or business that lost property in the Hatton Garden burglary earlier this year?'

They were also told the trial was expected to last around four weeks, though in the 'worst case scenario' it might not finish until 15 January 2016. In the event, it ended on the 14th.

The court went into recess and the prosecution did not begin until 23 November. In front of a packed courtroom, the prosecutor, Philip Evans, opened proceedings by saying: 'This case involves well-publicised events which took place between 2 April and 5 April – Easter Weekend – earlier this year. Over that weekend a group of men carried out a plan to steal from the basement area of a building in Hatton Garden, the jewellery district of central London.'

He told the jury: 'You may already be aware that a very substantial quantity of gold, jewellery, precious stones, cash and other items were stolen from the vault in the basement of a building at 88–90 Hatton Garden. During this trial you will hear evidence about the incident itself and also about the build-up, the planning, which went into this offence. You will hear who the Crown says was involved in the planning; who was at Hatton Garden; how the offence was committed and what happened afterwards to items they stole.'

Mr Evans went on to explain that the offence spanned much of the weekend in question. This was because, as would become clear from the evidence, the raid was only partially successful on the first night, 2 April. Consequently the burglars returned on 4 April with new equipment to finish off the job.

'You will appreciate that a criminal enterprise of this size and undoubted ambition not only involves an enormous amount of detailed planning but also a number of people, recruited to assist in various different ways,' he added. 'Some of those people may not actually have been at Hatton Garden over that weekend but despite that, they played a role in the criminal enterprise.'

This was the case with some of those on trial.

'These four defendants' roles began at different times,' he continued, 'and in some cases finished at different times, but nonetheless each of them played their part.'

The prosecutor then listed the three counts, or charges, that the jury would have to consider. The first was conspiracy to burgle. It was alleged that the defendants made an agreement to burgle the vaults of the safety deposit company in Hatton Garden. This dated from 17 May 2014. Evidence would show that, the following day, a computer belonging to one of the conspirators logged that enquiries were made about a suitable drill.

'That is the first realistic piece of evidence which shows not just an interest by one man in burgling such a vault, but of the plan actually forming,' said Mr Evans.

The second date on the indictment was 5 April 2015 at 7.30 a.m. This was approximately when the men left the scene of their crime for the last time. Mr Evans told the jury that they would only have to decide on this count in the case of the first three defendants: Wood, Lincoln and Harbinson.

'Count 2 relates to each of the four defendants and is an allegation that they conspired or agreed – with others – to conceal, convert or transfer criminal property,' he continued.

'You will see the dates are for a shorter period, encapsulating the period when this specific aspect of the plan was formed.'

He pointed out that the criminal property referred to in this count was the items stolen from the basement of the Hatton Garden Safe Depository. The allegation was that the people involved in this conspiracy agreed to, and played their own part in, concealing or hiding the proceeds of the burglary with a view to converting it to money or transferring it from one person or place to another. In other words, they had agreed to play their part in the laundering of the stolen property. All four defendants had to answer that charge.

'To convict a defendant on Count 2 you would need to be satisfied that when they agreed to play their part and, when they did what they did, they did so knowing or believing they were agreeing to deal with criminal property,' the prosecutor added.

He went on to explain that Count 3 was an 'alternative count' which applied to Doyle only. It alleged if he did not enter into a conspiracy to do so, he nevertheless participated in concealing, converting or transferring criminal property. This was a less serious allegation and would only be considered by the jury should Doyle be found not guilty on Count 2.

'The allegation relates to exactly the same crime,' said Mr Evans. 'The difference is that you could find Mr Doyle guilty of Count 3 if he only suspected he was dealing with criminal property – as opposed to Count 2, where his state of mind would need to be one of knowing or believing he was dealing with the criminal property.'

Mr Evans went on to explain the law on conspiracy. Its central premise was that two or more people came to an agreement to commit an offence, the jury was told, and that the individuals concerned should have the intention of taking part in the crime when the agreement was made.

The prosecutor then told the jury that others had already pleaded guilty to conspiracy to burgle, so it was beyond doubt that a conspiracy did take place.

'What those pleas do not confirm is that these defendants were a party to that conspiracy,' said Mr Evans. 'That remains very much an issue in this trial and it will be for the Crown to prove to you that they were.'

Those four men who had pleaded guilty to conspiracy to burgle had also been charged with conspiracy to conceal, convert or transfer criminal property – the subject of Count 2. But as they had pleaded guilty to burglary, the Crown had taken the view it was no longer in the public interest to continue with a trial against them in the other matter.

'Despite that, the Crown maintains they were also co-conspirators in Count 2 and some of the evidence against them will be produced in this trial so you can see it clearly demonstrates that fact,' said Mr Evans.

He then told the jury about the four who had already pleaded guilty. The first was seventy-four-year-old John Kenneth Collins, known by his co-conspirators as 'Kenny'. He was a ringleader and was present at the numerous face-to-face meetings with the others, both before and after the burglary.

Collins visited Hatton Garden a number of times to check out the premises and the surrounding area. Mr Evans alleged that Collins recruited Lincoln and Harbinson, with whom he had family ties. Collins lived with Lincoln's sister and recruited him along with Harbinson, who was Lincoln's nephew. Evidence would show that Harbinson visited Hatton Garden in February. Collins also recruited Hugh Doyle, whom he appeared to know well. And Collins drove a white Mercedes, car registration number CP13 BGY.

'That is a car you will see on a number of occasions during the evidence in this case,' added the prosecutor.

Not only had Collins recruited the others, Evans said, 'He visited Hatton Garden on a number of times in the build-up to this offence, no doubt to check out the premises and surrounding areas. He was the lookout during the course of the burglary and his role was also to drive the van to and from the scene.'

When his home address in Bletsoe Walk, Islington, North London, was searched, a large amount of cash, wristwatches, coins, jewellery and a money counter were found, Mr Evans said.

Another of the ringleaders was sixty-year-old Daniel Jones.

'He was at the heart of the extensive planning and had regular meetings with others, both before and after the Easter weekend,' said Mr Evans.

These took place on Friday nights in various meeting places, such as a public house called the Castle, off the Pentonville Road in Islington. The chief players would have a Friday-night drink there while planning the Hatton Garden burglary.

'As part of that planning phase, Jones was frequently in contact, both face-to-face and on the telephone, with Carl Woods, updating him on the plan,' said Mr Evans. 'Jones was at the burglary throughout and was instrumental in gaining access to the vault, and after the first-night failure, he, with Collins, obtained further equipment to do so.'

He lived on Park Avenue in Enfield.

'You can see Mr Jones's black Land-Rover. You can see Mr Jones's house,' said the prosecutor. 'You can see some of the things that were found at his house – including facemasks; a drill and uncounted cash; a book called *Forensics for Dummies*, a walkie-talkie, which was used to communicate during the burglary, and a magnifying glass.'

The book was crucial. It promised to show how to 'assess the scene of a crime, analyse trace evidence [and] pursue a career in forensics'. In the vault, no fingerprints or other forensic traces were found. He had also buried some of the stolen goods in a cemetery in Edmonton. Jones had been at the heart of the extensive planning, Mr Evans said.

The third ringleader was sixty-seven-year-old Terrence Perkins, who had been present at meetings both before and after the burglary. He was also present throughout the raid and was inside the building when it was burgled.

'Perkins was instrumental in the decision taken to use Mr Harbinson to transport the stolen property, because of the fact that Mr Harbinson was a taxi driver,' said Mr Evans. 'Importantly, he lives near Jones in Enfield.'

While planning the heist, Perkins and Collins often met in Scotti's Snack Bar in Clerkenwell, close to Hatton Garden, the jury were told. Meanwhile, Jones kept Wood informed on the 'developing plan as it gathered speed'. It was also thought that Perkins was responsible for checking out the gang's way into the vaults via the elevator shaft. Two days earlier he had been seen dressed as a lift engineer by staff, who believed he was carrying out repairs.

When Perkins's home on Heene Road, Enfield, was searched, the police found jewellery, cash, blue overalls, five pairs of white fabric gloves and a quantity of euros.

'The fourth conspirator to have pleaded guilty is Brian Reader,' said Mr Evans. 'He was referred to by his co-conspirators as "The Guvnor" or "The Master" and was the oldest of the conspirators.'

Reader was seventy-six at the time of the burglary and was

involved in the planning. Again, he was present at the meetings before and after the burglary. He was in the building in Hatton Garden on the first night of the burglary, but not on the second night.

'He does not appear to have owned his own mobile phone and may have used his son Paul Reader's mobile to be in contact on occasions with his co-conspirators,' said Mr Evans.

This was what implicated Paul Reader in the conspiracy, though he was completely innocent.

'When I was arrested, I didn't even bother to ask for a lawyer,' he told *The Guardian*. 'I even asked, "What is this about?" I was dreading the interview, thinking it would be old-style, like *Life on Mars*, but it wasn't like that at all. I think they were graduates.'

He spent his time weeks in Belmarsh quietly reading David Jason's autobiography but, like his father, he was not a well man and his health deteriorated in prison. When he was taken to hospital, he was handcuffed and accompanied by ten armed officers, with a helicopter circling above. The armed officers insisted on being present for his CT scan, but the nurse was adamant. Eventually she told them they could stay – provided they stripped off. That worked and they backed off.

According to the prosecution when the Readers' property on Dartford Road, Dartford, was searched, the police found a book on the underworld diamond trade, a diamond tester, a diamond gauge, diamond magazines and a distinctive scarf, which he can be seen wearing on CCTV footage at Hatton Garden on the night of 2 April.

'These four ringleaders and organisers of this conspiracy, although senior in years, brought with them a great deal of experience in planning and executing sophisticated and serious acquisitive crime not dissimilar to this,' Mr Evans told the court.

'This offence was to be the largest burglary in English legal history. Two of these men had also been involved in some of the biggest acquisitive crimes of the last century, and the other two had for many years in their earlier lives been involved in serious theft.'

The prosecutor then turned to the matter of the ninth man – the one who got away. This was the redhead who could be seen on CCTV entering the premises by the front door and letting the others in through the fire escape. He had not been traced or captured.

'This man has not been identified,' said Mr Evans. 'He has become known simply as "Basil".' He is, says the Crown, the same man who entered 88–90 a few minutes earlier. Precisely how he earlier opened the door at street level is unclear, but it appears that once he had done so, he waited until Mr Wiffen [a jeweller who worked in the building] had left the premises before he then opened the fire-exit door to allow others in. To gain access to the courtyard, though, all that was required was to pull back the two bolts on the basement door; the door to the staircase from the ground-floor lobby was never locked.'

Mr Evans explained why he had outlined the involvement of the other men who were not on trial. It was necessary for the jury to appreciate the scale of the conspiracy.

'This is important for you to understand because it demonstrates that men with that level of experience, engaged in a crime of this complexity and severity, would only have involved those who could be fully trusted,' he said. 'Collins knew that he could trust Lincoln, Harbinson and Doyle and could vouch for them to the others. Wood, as one of those the Crown says was physically present at the burglary, must have been very trusted by these individuals.'

The prosecutor acknowledged that some of those in the dock were not accused of taking part in the burglary itself, but they had helped afterwards: 'You will appreciate that a criminal enterprise of this size and undoubted ambition not only involves an enormous amount of detailed planning but also a number of people, recruited to assist in various different ways,' he said. 'These four defendants' roles began at different times and in some cases finished at different times but nonetheless each of them played their part in this enterprise, which took place at Hatton Garden.'

The gang had stolen around £14 million in jewels, precious metals and cash, Mr Evans added. Two-thirds of it had yet to be recovered. While lower-value goods had been found, many loose precious stones were still missing, along with quantities of precious metals. They were thought to be worth around £9 million. However, the court was told, it had been difficult to work out exactly how much had been taken.

'The calculation of that figure continues and may change again due to the massive scale of the task but it is currently estimated, and I stress estimated, to be just short of £14 million,' said Evans.

The jury was shown examples of the valuables recovered, including a tray of rings. They also saw the photographs that had been shown to the victims when they were asked to identify their property.

'The police have, as you will hear, recovered some of the property,' said the prosecutor. 'But as you may imagine, and unhelpfully, that property was not recovered in the same order it was taken nor was it labelled as to which box it had been taken from. It was taken by the burglars and lumped together in no particular order, no doubt to ease the huge logistical problem of getting it away from the scene. The police are left with thousands of items of jewellery, for example, hundreds of gold chains and rings, often similar in appearance, and many paper packages used in the jewellery trade – known as "brifkas" – containing individual precious stones.'

Some of the stolen items were promptly reunited with their owners. Others proved to be more difficult to identify and sometimes different people laid claim to them. It was the more expensive items, along with a large amount of cash, which still seemed to be missing.

'The process is now into its next stage, that of showing the victims each of the actual items of jewellery to see if more certainty can be established, perhaps with the use of identifying marks,' said Evans. 'What has become apparent from this process is that the items, which have been recovered, are in the main the lower-value items that were stolen. It appears, for example, that higher-value items and many loose precious stones are not among the property recovered. Also in the burglary a quantity of bullion was stolen. That amounted to, for example, gold, platinum and other precious metal bars, ingots and coins.'

None of this precious metal had been recovered and while cash had been recovered from some of the defendants, they could not be sure that it had come from the raid since there was no record of the serial numbers of the missing money. The police had so far identified forty people whose valuables had been stolen.

'The process of identifying what has been recovered will be a long one and will take many months from now to complete,' added the prosecutor. 'Consequently, any figures you are given now can only be estimates but based upon such estimates of the losers themselves it is thought, at best, that approximately one third of the value of property taken may have been recovered.

THE GREAT DIAMOND HEIST

This leaves, somewhere in the world, a great deal of criminal property from Hatton Garden, which has been concealed, converted or transferred.'

CHAPTER THRITEEN

THE SCENE OF
THE CRIME

The jurors were shown where Hatton Garden Safety Deposit was on the map and Mr Evans described the premises. In the basement, there was a large vault door with a big Chubb lock, dating back to the 1940s, which opened with a dual combination and a key.

'As you walk in through that door, you enter a room or vault which contains 996 safety deposit boxes in four sizes, of which 562 were occupied in April 2015,' the prosecutor said. 'Within that vault there are also two walk-in safes. There is also a further walk-in safe outside the vault, accessed from the same corridor.'

The vault has seen little refurbishment since it was built. However, CCTV and intruder alarms had recently been installed. The vault was now owned by the Bavishi family, Mr Evans explained. The patriarch, Mahendra Bavishi, had been a director since 2001, although he had no day-to-day involvement as he lived in the Sudan. His son, Manish Bavishi, was solely responsible for the day-to-day running of the company. Another of Mahendra's sons, Alok Bavishi, looked after the company on his brother's instructions when he was out of the country. All three men were 25-per-cent shareholders. The fourth shareholder, with an equal share, was Mahendra Bavishi's wife.

The majority of the clientele were Hatton Garden jewellers. They rented a safety deposit box from the company and entered into a contract as a tenant. Mr Evans explained that the company had no right to access to the boxes except in certain exceptional circumstances. What was inside them was private and known only to the tenants.

Daily business in the vault was carried out by two full-time security guards: Kelvin Stockwell, who had been there over twenty years, and Keefa Kamara, who had worked there for over twelve years. Both had access to the building, the alarm and the vault. Manish Bavishi only visited the property rarely as business commitments kept him elsewhere.

Large wooden street doors gave access to the premises. Inside was a set of magnetic doors and a lift to the basement, which had not been used for many years. Another door led to the stairs to the basement. Few people had keys to that door.

At the bottom of the stairs, the wooden door of the Hatton Garden Safe Deposit was immediately to the left. It was secured with a mortise deadlock that could not be slipped. There were only three people with keys to that door – the two security guards and Manish Bavishi.

The outer door was unlocked during opening hours. Anybody could reach it, unchallenged. But beyond it, anyone entering would have to get past the security guards. Once inside the wooden door, the person entering had 60 seconds to deactivate the intruder alarm. This was done by entering a five-digit code on the keypad of the alarm box.

If the intruder alarm was activated, the monitoring company contacted Manish Bavishi; if he could not be reached, they would get in touch with the security guards. They would then come and check out the building. In these circumstances, it was company policy that staff should never enter the vault alone.

There were two sliding metal gates that formed a so-called 'airlock'. The first was immediately behind the wooden door. It was locked magnetically and was opened from the outside by entering a four-digit code on the pin-code box. From the inside, it was opened either by pressing a foot switch under the power box, which was beneath the desk there, or by pressing two door-release buttons. The second sliding iron gate forming the other end of the airlock was locked manually with a key, as the magnetic lock had been removed due to a fault.

Within the airlock between the two sliding gates was a small office containing the CCTV recorder. This was known as the gated vent room. There was also a cupboard underneath the stairs housing the alarm panel. The cupboard door was never locked, but the door had to be closed for the alarm to be set. Then there was a locked shutter in the airlock. Behind it were the doors to the disused lift.

'The reason it was disused was because Mr Stockwell, the security guard, reports that the lift has not been used to access the basement since the 1970s, when a man with a shotgun used it to gain entry to the vault area,' Mr Evans explained. 'The only time these shutters are lifted is when the lift shaft requires cleaning or if another tenant has dropped keys or jewels down the shaft. The lift from the ground floor does not come down to the basement.'

The Chubb vault itself was opened by unlocking the combination locks and manually opening the door. The majority of the individual boxes were dual-locked – they could only be opened when both keys were used. But some had combination locks or used combination locks with keys. Only those renting boxes were allowed to enter the vault and they had to sign an entry book.

'Kelvin Stockwell does recollect, though, allowing potential customers – four or five in the last year – to look round the vault, and in those circumstances no record was kept,' Mr Evans added.

The main doors at street level were not the only way in. Mr Evans explained there was a second way to reach the basement and the wooden outer door to the vault area. This was from the fire exit opening out onto Greville Street.

'Through this second entrance are iron stairs leading down from street level to the courtyard adjoining the basement of 88–90 Hatton Garden,' he said. 'This door is usually locked with a key.'

The door from the courtyard to the basement had two sliding bolt locks, one on the top and one on the bottom, secured from the inside, outside opening hours.

The office of the jeweller Lionel Wiffen was also off that courtyard. When the main building was locked, clients visited him by going through the fire escape. He also used the door himself. There were only two holders of the keys to the Greville Street entrance – Lionel Wiffen himself and Hirschfields, the antique jewellers who had been in Hatton Garden for well over a century.

Security was provided by a communal CCTV, operated by the building owners. Two cameras covered the ground-floor area. Two further cameras covered the rear courtyard by the iron stairs to the Greville Street entrance. And a fifth camera covered the flat roof on the first floor.

'The monitor and the hard drive for the communal CCTV were located in Carlos Cruse's office, two doors away,' said Mr Evans. 'That CCTV was taken and is not available now. The hard drive was taken.'

The Safe Deposit had a separate CCTV system with five cameras. There were two inside the vault and two outside it. The fifth was training on the front door to the depository. But the recorder was in the cupboard within the airlock. It was also removed, so its footage was again not available.

'But the burglars did not realise that one camera which was inside the corridor from the fire exit passageway to Greville Street was not part of the building's CCTV but was on a separate system owned by a separate jeweller called Berganza,' said Mr Evans. 'They had a camera pointing over the back door to their premises.'

Their camera was triggered by movement so their system captured some of the arrivals and departures of the burglars. A separate business on the second floor of the building also had its own CCTV in the corridor; it filmed two men who briefly went to the second floor to deal with the lift.

The jury was also shown 3D images of Hatton Garden Safe Deposit showing the damage the burglars had wrought. The doors and gates were broken and the shutter to the basement lift access had been forced open.

Mr Evans told the jury that they would see all the relevant CCTV footage and photographs. There were maps showing where the defendants lived around London. Automatic Number Plate Recognition (ANPR) records tracking the movements of the suspects' cars would also be present in evidence, along with mobile phone records of the calls between the admitted conspirators and the defendants.

'There is no dispute in this trial that the phone numbers on that page are properly attributed and so your task will be to establish, not whether a phone was the property of the individual defendant or whether he was using it at the given time, but whether at that time the defendant was using that phone for the purpose which the Crown suggests,' said the prosecutor.

While the burglars had left no forensic trace at the scene of the crime, Mr Evans told the jury that a lot of the evidence in the case had come from mobile and landline telephones. Mobile phone records showed that the conspirators made frequent reconnaissance trips to the area.

'Importantly, after the burglary the police conducted visual surveillance of the conspirators and used recording equipment to record conversations which took place in two of the cars used by the conspirators,' he said. The devices were placed in Collins's white Mercedes and Perkins's Citroën Saxo.

After lunch, the prosecution began discussing the planning of the heist. Jurors were told that Mr Lionel Wiffen was a jeweller whose office is in the courtyard next to 88–90 Hatton Garden. He had been feeling 'uneasy' from January, four months before the raid took place.

'He felt that there were vehicles watching him or the fire escape on Greville Street,' Mr Evans explained. 'The prosecution's case is that he was right.'

'Long before what happened during two different nights in early April, these defendants met frequently, very often on a Friday, to discuss how the burglary was to be successfully carried off,' Mr Evans continued. 'It is clear that from the earliest stages Hatton Garden was the target. Collins, often with others, visited numerous times to assess the vault's weaknesses. The defendants' meeting places were normally only a short distance away from the jewellery quarter: they spent many hours talking and making plans at the Castle, a pub on Pentonville Road in Islington, and Scotti's, a nearby café.'

The raid had been at least three years in the planning. Conspirators had been carrying out Internet searches on specialist drills dating back to August 2012. By May 2014, they had narrowed the search down to the Hilti DD350 and watched YouTube clips showing how to operate it.

Using Excel spreadsheets projected onto screens in the courtroom, Mr Evans took the jury through a timetable showing how the conspiracy had developed. On 16 January, he told the jury, Jones and Collins were in the vicinity of the Castle public house, as they were most Friday evenings. Perkins was probably with them as he had called Collins before he met up with Jones.

'It is not possible to say where Wood was on the evening of 16 January because of an absence of any available cell site data,' explained Mr Evans, 'but the following morning, Wood and Jones spoke to one another, just before 10 a.m. for over two minutes.'

The prosecution case was that the matters discussed in the Castle between Jones, Collins and possibly Perkins were canvassed with others beforehand and then passed on to Wood after the meeting.

'There's a pattern which develops,' said Mr Evans.

He explained how mobile phone data could be used to follow the movements of the conspirators and alleged conspirators. Jones's phone was tracked to the area of the Castle that Friday, while Collins's car was tracked on the ANPR system.

Mr Evans then moved on to Friday, 23 January. Collins and Perkins, at least, were at the Castle pub again, he told the jury.

'Earlier that day, Perkins had been in contact with Brian Reader,' he said. 'At 6.10 p.m., when Collins and Perkins were together at the Castle public house, Perkins called Paul Reader's mobile phone for a period of one minute and three seconds to speak to Brian Reader.'

That call was made from a cell serving the Castle pub, and was the last call made between the conspirators that day. Collins was recorded driving away from the pub at 7.27 p.m. The following afternoon, Wood and Jones spoke for nearly four minutes.

On Friday, 12 February, there was another meeting between Jones and Perkins at the Castle, Mr Evans said. Following the meeting, Perkins's blue Citroën Saxo was seen in the vicinity of Hatton Garden before returning to Enfield.

The day before the meeting, Wood had spoken to Jones for three minutes and 36 seconds and, and the following morning they spoke on the phone once again,.

'On 14 February, Perkins travelled in his Citroën Saxo to an area consistent with him having visited London City Metals to visit a man the group referred to as "Frank",' said Mr Evans. 'This is a venue which the Crown says the conspirators planned – as confirmed in a later conversation in their cars – to be used to dispose of some of the items stolen from Hatton Garden. Later that day, once he had returned home, Jones called Perkins, no doubt to update him.'

Three days later, Jones and Collins 'conducted reconnaissance' in Hatton Garden. Collins was tracked on ANPR and Jones on his mobile. It was 'likely' that Perkins was with them, the prosecutor said. When Jones returned home, he called Wood.

'It was typical that Wood would be updated after a day's events during these months,' said Mr Evans, 'and this was almost always done by Jones.'

THE SCENE OF THE CRIME

Mobile phone evidence placed Collins near Hatton Garden for about an hour from 9 p.m. on 20 February, Mr Evans said. His Mercedes was then spotted crossing London Bridge, then at Old Street, back on the north side of the river.

'This detour was consistent with dropping Brian Reader back at London Bridge railway station so that he could catch a train back to Dartford, as he would subsequently do on 3 April 2015 in the midst of the burglary,' Mr Evans explained.

It seemed that on that day too Reader had come by public transport.

Collins's car was traced to Hatton Garden again on Tuesday, 24 February, before moving to the Castle pub. Mobile phone records placed Jones and Perkins in the vicinity of the Castle.

'The inference is that they met at the Castle, having conducted another site visit in Hatton Garden,' said Mr Evans.

This pattern continued throughout March, with Collins scouting Hatton Garden five times. Throughout, Wood, Jones and Perkins were in communication, both on the phone and at face-to-face meetings, the court heard. The three men were all traced to the same address in Islington on the afternoon of 20 March. But that evening they maintained 'radio silence' so their phones could not have been traced, the prosecutor said.

'The Crown's case is that late that evening and once Perkins and the others had joined Collins at Bletsoe Walk they all went to Hatton Garden, arriving at about 9.15 p.m.,' the court heard. 'The white Mercedes car left the area at around 9.40 p.m. and was back in the vicinity of Bletsoe Walk about five minutes later. About thirty-five minutes later, Mr Perkins car travelled along the A10 Great Cambridge Road, consistent with it returning home from Bletsoe Walk.'

Harbinson could also be tied in, Mr Evans told the court.

His phone was traced making long calls to Collins's address on Bletsoe Walk on 30 and 31 March.

Just three days before the burglary began, Harbinson spent over 36 minutes on the phone to the landline at Bletsoe Walk. This was the first time since 1 January that Harbinson could be shown to have called, or been called by, any of the conspirators, other than his uncle, Lincoln.

'It is fair to say that Jon Harbinson's aunt Millie Garrett also lives with Collins, at Bletsoe Walk, and a conversation with her can't be ruled out,' Mr Evans conceded.

But he was not to be deflected.

'However, his family relationships with both Collins and Lincoln perhaps demonstrate why he became trusted in such large-scale crime in the first place,' he alleged.

The prosecution went on to tell the court that a witness recalled an occasion around 31 March – she is not sure about the date – when the lift in 88–90 Hatton Garden took an unusually long time to come. When it finally arrived, after some six or seven minutes, a sixty-year-old man with white hair, wearing blue overalls, was inside, surrounded by tools and building equipment. It occurred to the witness that it would have been hard for him to get into the lift without someone loading the tools after him. He smiled apologetically, as there was no room for her to get in, and the doors closed.

'Perkins fits this description,' said Mr Evans. 'He was in the vicinity around this time and a pair of blue overalls was eventually seized from his house.'

By approximately 4 p.m. that afternoon Woods's phone was using a cell site situated just to the south of the North Circular, near the A10. Shortly after 4 p.m., Perkins's car registered on an ANPR device just to the north of the North Circular Road, also on the A10.

CHAPTER FOURTEEN

CALL TO ACTION

After a short break, Mr Evans took the jury through the events of the night of 2 April when the burglary began. That morning, Harbinson allegedly called Lincoln. Phone records put his call close to Collins's home in Bletsoe Walk at 11.28 a.m.

'The records of Brian Reader's Oyster card show his journey from Dartford, beginning with him boarding the 96 bus,' Mr Evans said. 'His Oyster then shows him exiting Waterloo East Station at 18.31 and by 19.02, boarding the 55 bus, which would take him to St John Street, about a five-minute walk from Hatton Garden, where, later, he would meet the rest of the group.'

There, the scene was unfolding.

'While Brian Reader was travelling, the security guards locked the vault. Kelvin Stockwell set the alarm as usual and the electric door was slid back,' explained Mr Evans. 'He was the last to leave, at about 6 p.m. It was the bank holiday Easter weekend. He and his colleague did not expect to return until Tuesday, 7 April.'

THE GREAT DIAMOND HEIST

Carlos Cruse, the building co-ordinator, checked the courtyard and the basement. Mr Evans said: 'He could see the Hatton Garden Safety Deposit security guards preparing to lock up. He waited for them to leave the building. Once they had gone, he activated the magnetic glass door and left through the main doors, which closed behind him and locked automatically.'

Mr Evans then took the jury through a series of CCTV still images.

'The white van was driven by a male, who the prosecution can now identify as John Collins – one of the men who has pleaded – arrived in the vicinity of Hatton Garden at approximately 8.20 to 8.25 p.m.,' he went on. 'The van parked in Leather Lane around the corner from 88–90 Hatton Garden. At around 8.28 p.m., two men, one of whom is Mr Jones and the other, the Crown says, is Mr Carl Wood, exit the van. For the purposes of the trial, the figure the Crown says is Wood will be known as Man F.'

Addressing the jury, Mr Evans said: 'You will have to decide – is it Carl Wood or not?'

His narration continued: 'Initially, they walked down Greville Street. They are walking around, observing the building in question and then walked around the block and back down Leather Lane, and back to the parked van. The man the Crown says is Mr Wood is dressed in dark clothing, with a hi-visibility waistcoat and navy baseball cap. He was also wearing a white surgeon's-style mask and dark gloves. He was carrying a black backpack.

'Later, in the CCTV, the same man was seen to be wearing glasses. He was with Mr Jones. Jones was dressed in a hooded jumper with white writing, striped trousers (although the stripes are not always visible in all CCTV shots), a hi-visibility waistcoat, red trainers and a navy baseball cap.'

CALL TO ACTION

Continuing to take the jury through stills from the CCTV, Mr Evans said a man could be seen walking along Greville Street, with a black bag on his shoulder. He went into the main door of 88–90 Hatton Garden. Man F – Wood – and Jones then left the van. Jones was seen standing on Greville Street opposite the fire-exit door by a telephone box. He appeared to have something to his ear, which was possibly a walkie-talkie, Mr Evans said.

The jury was told that jeweller Lionel Wiffen left his office at around 9.20 p.m.

'At about 9.22 p.m., CCTV shows a red-haired man with a hat on appearing in the courtyard from within 88–90 Hatton Garden, carrying what seems to be a black bin-bag slung over his shoulder to obscure the camera's view. What happened next is actually out of shot, but given his position and what he does, the only real inference from what follows is that he opened the fire-escape door from the inside.'

This man had not been identified.

'He has become known simply as "Basil". He is, says the Crown, the same man who entered 88–90 a few minutes earlier.'

The prosecution were still at a loss as to how he got in.

'Precisely how he earlier opened the door at street level is unclear,' Mr Evans went on, 'but it appears that once he had done so, he waited until Mr Wiffen had left the premises, before he then opened the fire-exit door to allow others in. To gain access to the courtyard, though, all that was required was to pull back the two bolts on the basement door; the door to the staircase from the ground-floor lobby was never locked.'

The CCTV then showed the white transit van arriving from the direction of Leather Lane.

'It stopped outside the fire escape,' said Mr Evans. 'Several men got out, and started to unload bags, tools and two wheelie bins, which they carried, or wheeled, in through the fire escape and down the stairs. Large metal joists were being ferried down the stairs: they would become important. These men were Brian Reader, Terence Perkins Daniel Jones and Man F, Carl Wood.'

Reader was distinguishable because of his stripy socks and brown shoes, along with a scarf that would eventually be seized from his home address at Pentire.

'He also wore a yellow hard hat and a hi-visibility jacket with "GAS" written on the back,' Mr Evans added. 'Perkins was dressed in dark clothing, with a hi-visibility waistcoat, a yellow hard hat and a white surgeon's-style mask.'

Jones was dressed in a hooded jumper with white writing, striped trousers, a hi-visibility waistcoat, red trainers and a navy baseball cap. Later, in CCTV footage, he was seen using a walkie-talkie. 'Man F', allegedly Wood, was wearing dark clothing, with a hi-vis jacket and navy baseball cap, along with glasses, a white medical-style mask and dark gloves, and carrying a black rucksack. Collins was wearing a flat cap and carrying a briefcase.

After the jury had been shown the CCTV footage of the thieves arriving in a white van and then entering the building through a fire escape, which had been opened for them by 'Basil', Mr Evans said: 'The white van then moved off, continued round the block, and parked in Cross Street. John Collins got out and walked to the back of the vehicle. It appears that the burglars had forgotten something in the van as he was joined by Daniel Jones, who had run to where it was parked, from 88–90. Jones collected a green crate and returned to the fire escape; he carried it, then the wheelie bins, down the stairs, assisted by Man F – Carl Wood.'

Philip Evans continued: 'Collins can be seen walking along Hatton Garden to the crossroads with Greville Street, wearing a green quilted jacket, a flat cap and carrying a brown briefcase; he then went into 25 Hatton Garden. How he got in is not altogether clear, but he spent some time at the door of the property as if he is trying to open it. There is no question that there was at that time an abundance of keys to the main door of these premises in circulation. Studios and offices inside 25 Hatton Garden afford a clear view of both doors to 88–90 Hatton Garden, which now had Perkins, Reader, Jones and Wood inside. Collins positioned himself there as a lookout for his co-conspirators.'

Mr Evans noted that throughout the entire time they were at Hatton Garden the defendants and the admitted conspirators did not make or receive any mobile phone calls. The gang communicated with Collins, the lookout, by walkie-talkie, the jury was told, rather than their mobile phones, which they knew could be used to track their movements.

Reader, Perkins, Jones and Wood began to unload bags, tools, large metal joists and two wheelie bins. They then carried the equipment through the fire escape and down the stairs.

While there was no CCTV to show what happened next, Mr Evans continued his narration.

'The lift car had been moved to the second floor, where it had been disabled: the door sensors had been left hanging off so that the doors would remain open,' he said. 'This opened a short drop down the shaft from the ground floor to the basement.'

A handwritten note had been stuck next to the lift, which had not been there before: it said, 'Out of order'. At the bottom of the shaft, the shutters were then forced open from the inside, leaving them buckled.

'One or more of the four men crawled out of the lift shaft, which is located in the airlock to the cupboard beneath the stairs, and cut the grey telephone line cable coming out of the alarm box,' said Mr Evans. 'The GPS aerial had been broken off, significantly reducing the signal range. After attacking the alarm, the cover on the electrical box underneath the desk was removed and the wires were cut. This stopped the power to the iron gate, allowing it to be pulled open; the manual key-operated door release does not appear to have been touched. The lock was broken off the wooden door to Hatton Garden Safe Deposit, leaving a hole in it. This allowed access for larger machinery and easier passage to and from the vault.'

Without CCTV footage it was impossible to be accurate about the timing.

'It is likely that the outer iron gate was opened soon after midnight,' said Mr Evans. 'It is possible to establish an approximate time because at 00.18, the alarm finally managed to send an SMS message to the monitoring company: opening the outer door is likely to have improved the signal to the panel.'

Alok Bavishi received a call from the monitoring company almost immediately.

'He was told that the alarm was signalling and that the police were on scene,' explained Mr Evans. 'The latter part of the message was wrong – the police never came until later. Alok Bavishi rang Keefa Raymond Kamara, but the trains had stopped running and he was without a car, so he could not attend. He then rang Kelvin Stockwell. The call initially went to voicemail but after a few minutes it connected. He spoke to Stockwell, who agreed to go to Hatton Garden. Alok Bavishi himself was not originally intending to accompany him, but then decided he would as Stockwell was by himself and the police had been called, or at least he thought they had.'

What happened next was again caught on camera.

'At 00.51, Wood appeared in view of the CCTV camera at

the top of the basement stairs,' Mr Evans continued. 'He waited for a moment and then returned back down to the basement. Stockwell arrived at Hatton Garden at about 01.15. He called Alok Bavishi, who was by then five minutes away, to say that the main door and the fire exit appeared secure. He informed him, wrongly, that it was a false alarm. Both men returned home, as the attempts to access the vault, unbeknownst to them, continued inside.'

Throughout, the thieves were out of sight below ground.

'Uninterrupted thereafter, the men spent the night cutting through the second sliding iron gate and then drilling three adjoining and circular holes in the thick wall of the main vault with the Hilti DD350 drill they had brought with them,' Mr Evans went on. 'Their efforts left a 25cm by 45cm breach in the wall. They would, at this point, have encountered the back of the heavy metal cabinet housing the safe deposit boxes, which was fixed both to the floor and ceiling. It appears that they had with them on that first night a Clarke pump and hose, which included a 10-ton hydraulic ram; for some reason, though, the burglary was not completed that night. It seems, from what happened in the following days, that there was a problem with the pump and hose; what that problem was is not immediately clear, but it seemed it did not do its job and stopped them from moving the metal cabinet, bolted to the floor.'

It seemed the hydraulic ram was faulty. That was why they had to leave and return, two nights later, with new equipment to finish the job.

'It is clear from the evidence that the enterprise was only partially successful on the first night, 2 April, and the burglars returned on the 4 April with new equipment to finish the job,' said Mr Evans.

After the first night of the burglary, Reader was driven to London Bridge Station by Lincoln from Collins's home, Mr Evans said.

'This series of acts by Lincoln is, said the Crown, very significant,' Mr Evans insisted. 'The Crown says the timing of these visits, generated as they are by short calls, which were simply not long enough for Collins to have explained the plan, demonstrate that Lincoln was "in the know" before the burglary took place, and he had therefore entered the agreement before 7.30 a.m. on 5 April. The prosecution contend that he was connected to the conspiracy by ferrying gang members to meetings.'

Mr Evans continued: 'Having agreed to be a party to the conspiracy he agreed that his role would be as a getaway driver for the stolen property. No doubt, says the Crown, had the burglary been successful on the first night, Mr Lincoln would have collected the goods, as he clearly anticipated he was going to, and he would then have called up Jon Harbinson, in the way he subsequently did on April 5/6, who would have taken them further way under the disguise of his taxi.

'Jon Harbinson, says the Crown, was at this time also in the know, and was waiting for a call which, at that stage, didn't come because the burglars had not managed to get the jewellery and had no need at that stage for Jon Harbinson. Instead of taking the stolen goods away, Mr Lincoln provided a lift to Brian Reader.'

The prosecution further contended that, on 3 April, Jones and Collins travelled out to Twickenham in South-West London to buy more equipment to finish the burglary. There, they visited two shops – Machine Mart and D&M Tools. They did not buy anything at D&M Tools, but Machine Mart next door had records of selling a Clarke pump and hose – part of a car-body repair kit – to a 'V Jones' of Park Avenue, Enfield, Middlesex.

CALL TO ACTION

That was his home address and his partner's name was Valerie, although it was thought that he fancied himself as footballer-turned-film-star Vinnie Jones.

'Why the second pump and hose was required is not clear,' Mr Evans said. 'One possibility is that the base was shattered on the first night, which apparently can happen if it is not exactly perpendicular when in use. It is difficult to purchase an individual part and of course these customers were limited for time, so it was an entirely new kit that needed to be secured.'

Parts of a similar pump were found at the scene. It was thought they were damaged, preventing the burglary from being completed on the first night.

A series of phone calls were exchanged between the men. Then Collins drove Jones, and allegedly Wood, to Hatton Garden at around 9.20 p.m.

'Brian Reader, on this occasion, was nowhere to be seen,' said Mr Evans, 'and it appears that he had decided he no longer wanted any part in the activities at Hatton Garden.'

But Reader did not sever his connections with the heist completely: he was spotted by police surveillance officers with his partners-in-crime in the weeks after the raid. Some twelve days after the robbery, he was with Collins when they were photographed examining the contents of a bag.

The others first checked out the area in Collins's Mercedes, then returned in the white van about forty minutes later. 'Basil' then let the men into the building once more, after Lionel Wiffen had left.

'Importantly, whilst Basil was inside Hatton Garden, Mr Wood appears to go to the fire escape door – which Mr Wiffen had locked – and try it on a couple of occasions,' said the prosecutor. 'There then followed what appears to be a discussion in the street between the three men, Mr Wood, Mr Jones and Mr Collins. It appears from the CCTV as if Mr Wood then exits the area to the left of Leather Lane. The man the Crown says is Mr Wood is not seen again on the CCTV and it appears for whatever reason he decided at this point that he wanted out and he left the scene.'

Wood broke off all contact with other gang members, the court was told. It appeared that he had quit the team after finding that a door that the gang had anticipated would be open was unexpectedly locked. Mr Evans said Wood's withdrawal from the conspiracy was confirmed by conversations later recorded in Collins's white Mercedes and Perkins' Citroën Saxo. Before reading from the transcripts, Mr Evans apologised to the jury.

'You will forgive me if I don't get the intonation quite right,' he said.

He also warned jurors that Perkins's speech was quite graphic and he did not 'mince his words'.

On 15 May, Perkins and Jones were with Collins in his Mercedes when Perkins described how Wood had lost his nerve. Evans read from the transcript, quoting Perkins: 'He thought we would never get in, cause even the c*** . . . I said "give it another half hour. F***, we've done everything we can do, if we can't get in, we won't be able to get in, will we?"'

Mr Evans said: 'They were suggesting that Carl had lost his nerve.'

Perkins was also uncomplimentary about Doyle, who was accused of allowing the gang to use his premises: 'He ain't got a f***ing brain, has he?'

The jury was told that after Wood had left the vault, Basil appeared again and unlocked the fire-escape door. The others went back into the building, while Collins resumed his duties at lookout. CCTV footage then showed Jones carrying a black holdall and a red box. This was thought to have contained the pump and hose Jones had bought in Twickenham.

'Where the last attempt had been unsuccessful, the inference is that this time, with the second pump and hose, they accessed the vault by pushing over the cabinet,' said Mr Evans. 'In order to do that, they used the metal joists which they had taken in on the first night to anchor the pump and hose on the wall opposite the vault.'

After entering the vault and ransacking the safe deposit boxes, Jones emerged from the building at around 5.45 a.m. on 5 April.

'Perkins soon joined him and together they brought the two wheelie bins and several bags, all full of jewels and other valuable items, up the stairs to the fire escape,' said Mr Evans. 'This, no doubt due to the weight of the bins, did not prove to be an altogether straightforward task.'

Collins got the white van and drove it around to the fire escape, where Perkins and Jones loaded the wheelie bins, which were 'obviously very heavy', and other items into it. The thieves later split up the proceeds and went their separate ways, after agreeing to wait for the publicity to subside before trying to cash in.

'When they were confident that had happened, they could split it up, melt it down, sell it or hide it for a rainy day,' Mr Evans explained. 'Ultimately, however, their plan was to convert their criminal property into money.'

CHAPTER FIFTEEN

BUGGED AND BUSTED

Two weeks after the robbery, gang members were under police surveillance and were being bugged. From 17 April, they were observed regularly meeting in pubs, cafés and restaurants around London. They continued to meet at the Castle too. Flying Squad detectives were then filming their meetings, even using a lip-reader who watched as Perkins appeared to explain how they had used a hydraulic pump in the raid. He told his alleged co-conspirators: '. . . yeah, but he went down . . . to find a pump . . . boom . . . OK, a big one . . . . and so you wind everything around . . . the whole, the whole thing becomes smaller.'

Mr Evans told the jury: 'Perkins was clearly explaining the operation of the pump and hose and the noise of the cabinets falling over. Brian Reader had not been present on the second night, so would not have known in detail what had taken place.'

In a conversation recorded on 15 May, referring to either Wood or Reader, Jones said to Collins and Perkins: 'Yeah, well, that's my fault with him anyway. I said to him to stay there – if we get nicked, at least we can hold our heads up that we had a last go. And he goes "F***ing right," and what's he do . . .' Then Jones blew a raspberry.

The men in the car also described Reader and Wood as 'idiots' for pulling out of the job prematurely, when 'common sense' suggested they would eventually get into the vault.

'Never give up,' said Collins. 'The old saying comes round, never give up.'

Later in the conversation, Perkins told the others he was sorry he had not taken a selfie during the raid.

'I wish I had a photo, Dan,' he said. 'I know you and Basil was inside. I wish I had a photo to show me sat outside all on my own, right, doing what I had to do, to say to him, "That's where you left me, Brian, look, all OK on my own."'

On 18 May, Perkins and Jones were recorded discussing the breaching of the vault wall, where they had done the bulk of the work. Before the recordings were played, Judge Christopher Kinch told Woolwich Crown Court: 'There are some colourful sections and some choice language.'

According to the transcript, Perkins said: 'I mean, they have got to be two feet thick, ain't they?'

Jones said it was more than that.

'So they put the work down to me and you, they was sitting, going, "Put a bit here, try a bit there",' he continued.

'And you said, "Smash that up now, put that down",' said Perkins. 'It's f***ing working, cos you're egging one another on, going, "It's working, it's working, you got to take it off, it ain't pinging back." Remember me saying that "It ain't f***ing come back, we're in, we're in," and then you started pumping again, "Get some more, get some more." Ain't it?'

Jones was also recorded boasting about the size of the burglary and the coverage it was getting in the media.

Using the Cockney rhyming slang 'tom' – tomfoolery – for jewellery, he said: 'The biggest cash robbery in history at the time and now the biggest tom history in the f***ing world, that's what they are saying ... What are the odds? And what a book you could write. F***ing hell!'

During one conversation, Perkins asked how much he thought one of the items was worth. Jones replied: 'Two grand; two and a half grand; eighteen hundred quid; fourteen hundred quid. Sellable, yes, necklaces – all stone ones, few of them. Few of those bracelets ones, then you got the necklace with the f***ing big emeralds in it with the matching earrings. Another one there, they look nice . . . put stones in them, the necklace. Must be a couple hundred rings in there, but he's got a wrap like that, two of them full of rings and big diamond rings there.'

They could also be heard discussing gold, 12-carat diamonds and coins, while 'Kenny' was said to have been 'f***ed 24–7'.

Of the 18-carat Indian gold they had stolen, Perkins said: 'I'm going to melt my good gold down . . . The Indian, the 18, that could be my pension if I could get half an idea of what's there, you know what I mean . . .'

Later, Asian necklaces, bangles and pendants were recovered.

During the conversations they referred to 'Carl', 'Bill', 'Hughey' and 'The Taxi Driver'. The prosecution maintained that 'Carl' was Carl Wood, 'Bill' was William Lincoln, 'Hughey' was Hugh Doyle and 'The Taxi Driver' was Jon Harbinson.

In one extract, Perkins said it was good that the police thought the raid was an inside job.

'No, they can't work that out. That is the biggest robbery that could have ever, ever been,' he said.

'Yeah,' said Jones.

'That will never happen again.'

'No,' said Jones.

'The biggest robbery in the f***ing world, Dan,' Perkins continued, 'we was on that c***!'

Perkins said that, with his share of the haul, he had at least paid for his daughter's holiday and made sure she was all right.

'Not all I wanted to give them, but let's see what we got once we chop it up,' he went on. 'We will have half a clue. You can't plan on doing anything until you know what you got, can you?'

Perkins, who celebrated his sixty-seventh birthday during the robbery, was convinced that the police would never believe that a bunch of old men could have pulled it off. And if detectives did come knocking at his door…

'I'll say, "You what, you dopey c***? I can't even f***ing walk!"'

The men later appeared to make reference to another robbery, with Jones saying that Perkins had seen enough money in his life.

'A million pound out of the airport … f***ing hell!' Jones was recorded as saying.

Perkins replied: '£6 million out of there, f*** me!'

They also joked about giving back £1.6 million worth of gold and £70,000 in notes that they said was taken from a victim.

In another conversation played to the jurors, the men referred again to Wood, saying that he'd been 'squealing like a f***ing pig' after pulling out of the raid on the second night.

Jones said: 'He must be cursing himself, that c***!'

'Who?' asked Perkins.

'That Carl,' replied Jones. 'I'd be absolutely devastated, I would.'

'He must be thinking of committing suicide,' said Perkins. 'I wouldn't know what to do, Dan, now, if I were him. I would be the horriblest c*** in the world to live with.'

But there was no sympathy.

'I can't get over him, the c***,' Perkins continued. 'He's done me out of f***ing money. I'm trying to put myself in his mind . . . I bet he's boozing now . . . unless he has seen the light.'

In another extract, they talked about Bill and The Taxi Driver.

'I've been thinking, how the f*** has that Bill got involved? Another two people know, Bill and The Taxi Driver,' Perkins said.

In their conversations, they also referred to 'The Master' – Reader, the prosecution contended.

'The biggest cash robbery in history at the time and now the biggest tom in the fucking world, that's what they are saying,' Jones said. 'And if you listen to The Master, you walk away – The Master.'

Jones then referred to Reader as 'an old ponce'.

'All them months and f***ing years he's put work in, to go: "Look, I won't be here tomorrow." Cos he's thought you'll never get in,' said Jones. 'I really want to have a go at him, but I've got to stop myself. Really want to hit him and say, "Toughen up, you f***ing prick – that's what you are, you lost all the f***ing work, you bottle out at the last minute."'

Perkins added: 'The whole twelve years I've been with him, three, four bits of work, f***ed everyone of them.'

'And he would have f***ed this if we walked away with him,' said Jones.

Perkins said he planned to confront 'The Master'.

'I am going to say, "You f***ed up every one of them up, Brian, you didn't even look at the front door, you didn't take the right drill in and this one, you f***ing walked away from! If we had took any notice of you, we would have walked away from it as well."'

They were disgruntled.

Perkins said: 'We should be sitting here now . . .'

'. . . with half a billion pounds,' said Jones, finishing the sentence.

'With chauffeur-driven Bentleys . . .'

'One for every day. And all of them months and f***** years he put work in to go, "Look, I won't be here tomorrow". Cos he thought "Them c***s, you'll never get in there".'

Perkins went on to say: 'I have to say that in my opinion that to be true, he's a c***. He might have been years ago, but he's no value in my f***** eyes.'

'Everything he has done has f***** up,' Jones added

Wood was not treated with such utter contempt although he had walked away on the second night. In the same conversation in the car, Collins said: 'Carl's different, his arsehole went.'

For old men with medical conditions, the burglary had been something of a strain.

'Twenty pills a day, think of it – three injections. I had it all with me, my injections,' he told Perkins. 'Yeah, if I don't take insulin for three days, you'd have had to carry me out in a wheelie bin.'

Perkins was also heard asking Jones: 'The stones, where did you put them? Over the cemetery?'

Gang members were grasping that others had been brought in to hide and dispose of the proceeds. It was also clear that the loot was divided unequally, which became 'the subject of considerable controversy and intense discussion,' Mr Evans said. 'The circle, by now, had widened beyond the original circle of trust. This widening made its original members increasingly nervous.'

After lying low for several weeks, members of the gang met at a car park outside the Old Wheatsheaf pub in Enfield, next to Doyle's workshop, to divide up the loot.

Jurors were shown CCTV of the area around the pub on 18 and 19 May. On 18 May, Collins was seen parked in a lay-by in Chase Green, Enfield, close to Doyle's workshop. He was with his dog, Dempsey, and Perkins, Jones and Lincoln were seen milling round the car park. The footage showed Doyle getting out of his work van and walking up to Collins's white Mercedes.

In a covert police recording played to the jury, a man with an Irish accent, which was said to be Doyle, was recorded as saying: 'Can you tell me what you need, cos we have options.'

Ten minutes later, he was recorded saying: 'Give me two minutes, I'll try and get rid of Dave. I'll tell him to go get a coffee or something.'

Then Doyle walked towards a car park at the back of the Old Wheatsheaf pub, where his workshop was. Collins was then seen walking a dog in nearby Chase Gardens.

Mr Evans then told the jury: 'Mr Doyle comes back out.'

He was seen walking towards the park.

'Some minutes later, Mr Doyle went back towards his premises,' said Mr Evans.

Later, Doyle's vehicle was seen driving away towards Enfield town centre.

The CCTV footage from the following day was said to show stolen goods being transferred from Harbinson's silver Mercedes taxi into Collins's white Mercedes.

'Lincoln and Harbinson did not physically meet up immediately prior to the exchange, which is evidence that Harbinson had control of the property during the days leading up to the exchange,' explained Mr Evans. 'The conspirators chose to use the area outside Hugh Doyle's workshop because a boot-to-boot transfer would, they feared, look too obvious and ran the risk of detection. They were recorded expressing concern that the "Old Bill" might see them and so they needed somewhere to exchange, which was discreet.'

The court was told that the plan was to take the loot to an address linked to Perkins in Sterling Road, Enfield, and divvy it up there. Doyle was not present at the time of the exchange.

Wearing a red hoodie, Lincoln arrived at the scene in his black Audi A3, which was later stopped by police on the A10. He was boxed in by unmarked police cars, pulled out of the car, forced onto the road and arrested by plainclothes officers. Detective Constable Matthew Benedict said the car window was smashed during the arrest and it may have been 'frightening'.

Jurors were told that Lincoln was leaning down towards the centre console of the car when he was stopped. DC Benedict told the court: 'There was a pile of torn-up paper to the right-hand side, on the floor.'

Jurors were told that the torn-up note contained the handwritten address of the Old Wheatsheaf pub in Enfield.

DC Benedict said after smashing the window, he walked around the car and saw Lincoln in the footwell.

'He was on the floor,' DC Benedict explained. 'He was complaining of problems with his hips – said he had had a double-hip replacement.'

Lincoln was also incontinent, the jury heard. He said he had a 'weak bladder' and was assisted over to a bush at the side of the road to relieve himself before being taken back to Wood Green police station.

The detective told jurors that once in the custody suite, he informed other officers that the sixty-year-old was incontinent and would need to go to the toilet.

'They said he could not go to the toilet at the moment because it was busy,' DC Benedict said. 'And by the time I came back, he had already wet himself.'

Another of the arresting officers, Detective Constable Stephen O'Connell, said he saw a walking stick in the car. Lincoln also said he suffers from sleep apnoea, a condition where the sufferer ceases to breathe while asleep. DC O'Connell said it was plain he was 'unwell'.

Mark Tomassi, defending Lincoln, then asked O'Connell what he noticed about Lincoln.

'He was older, an old gentleman in his sixties, his size – he was a large guy,' the officer replied.

'I'm going to suggest during the period of time Mr Lincoln was at Wood Green police station, he asked police several times if he might be able to use the lavatory,' said Mr Tomassi.

'I don't remember that,' DC O'Connell said.

'And for one reason or another, this was not able to be achieved, causing him to wet himself. Do you remember that?' Mr Tomassi continued.

'I don't really remember that, no,' said O'Connell.

Lincoln was allowed to clean himself up and was given a fresh set of clothes, the officer said, before police went to his home to collect his medication and arranged for him to see a doctor.

Lincoln claimed that the car belonged to his wife and was used to transport his mother and mother-in-law. During the arrest, the police seized £467.02 in cash – including nine £50 notes, one £10 note, a £5 note and small change – as well as the Karrimor walking shoes he was wearing.

The court was told that, during a search of the Harbinson's home, they found the book *Killer*, the autobiography of career criminal Charlie Seiga, whose nickname was 'Killer'. A page was earmarked, where an attempt to drill into a vault was described. The Crown maintained that Harbinson, a black-cab driver and Lincoln helped move and conceal the haul.

Ring mounts, sovereigns and gold were found at Harbinson's house in Benfleet, the court was told. Plastic bags full of jewellery were hidden under a floorboard, in a loudspeaker, and behind a kitchen cupboard, and two Cartier and one Loewe watch behind a kickboard at the base of the kitchen units, the police said.

Exhibits officer Detective Sergeant Jim Simmons told the jury that officers were directed to the jewellery by Harbinson's partner, Cherie Wright.

Asked if she knew who they belonged to, she replied: 'To be honest, I haven't seen them before. I know his dad collects rings.'

She later added: 'Actually, they might have been his grandad's.'

The prosecution maintained that it was part of the haul.

When the stash from the car park of the Old Wheatsheaf arrived at Perkins's house, Flying Squad detectives who had been following the suspects moved in to make arrests. Jones, Perkins and Collins were found with three holdalls packed with a 'vast quantity' of gold and jewels: they had been caught red-handed.

The jury was then told that Jones's offer to show the police where he had hidden his share of the loot was disingenuous. They deliberately delayed taking him out of prison, ostensibly making arrangements for his security. Meanwhile, they were pursuing their own inquiries. These led them to plot GB800 in Edmonton Cemetery. Interred there was Sidney James Hart, the father of Valerie Hart, mother of Jones's children, the court was told. On 8 October, after lifting off the memorial stone, the police dug down and found two bags of rings and stones hidden in the mud, worth up to £55,000 each.

'There were two bags: one blue, which was sealed with tape,

and one red, orange and white, which contained a large quantity of jewellery,' Mr Evans told the jury. 'When the blue bag was opened, it was found to contain many packets or brifkas, which each appeared to contain precious stones.'

The police did not tell Jones what they had found. A week later, they did take him out of prison, according to the prosecution.

'Mr Jones directed the police, perhaps unsurprisingly, to the same cemetery in Edmonton,' said Mr Evans. 'He then identified an area of the cemetery and a memorial stone.'

It was the same cemetery, but a different memorial stone. This one was for another family member, Sidney John Hart, in plot GB177. There, they found hidden a smaller amount of gold and jewels.

'Underneath the memorial stone Mr Jones revealed what appeared to be a black and orange bag. That bag has now been opened and found to contain various items of gold and jewellery and a much smaller number of packets or brifkas containing precious stones,' Mr Evans continued. 'Mr Jones then told the police that he was the only person who knew it was there, and, importantly, he said there was no other outstanding property. He was then specifically asked whether there was anywhere else the police needed to go in order to recover property, and he replied, "That's all I had. The rest of it you got on the day."'

Jones was then returned to the prison.

'Mr Jones did not therefore tell the police of the existence of plot GB300 because he was hoping if he gave up the smaller quantity at plot GB177, he would still have access to the larger stash of criminal property, no doubt for his future use,' Mr Evans alleged.

At a house in Sterling Road where Jones, Perkins and Collins had been nicked, the police found three black holdalls stuffed with a large quantity of jewels, including sapphires and diamonds, Breitling, Omega, TAG Heuer and Rolex watches, ruby and emerald rings worth £15,000, a diamond ring worth £55,000, earrings, necklaces, bangles and brooches. Other items were marked 'Not for Sale'. A pot full of Asian necklaces, bangles and pendants was found, along with a smelter suitable for melting down precious metals. Crucibles and tongs used for smelting gold were discovered in a washing machine.

At William Lincoln's home in Winkley Street, a bag of jewellery was found behind the skirting board, another in the cupboard under the stairs, and banknotes were stashed under the microwave.

The plan was to convert the stolen goods into money, but initially they divided the haul between them. Their intention was to keep it hidden until publicity surrounding the burglar had died down, the court was told.

'They had to do something with it, they had to – in short – launder it,' explained Mr Evans. 'What they chose to do was to conceal it or hide it for a period of time until the tide of publicity had subsided and they hoped they would have avoided detection. When they were confident that had happened, they could split it up, melt it down, sell it or hide it for a rainy day.'

More was found in Jones's brother's loft. The prosecutor said: 'Some remained stashed behind skirting boards and in kitchen cupboards in the co-defendants' houses; some had already, by that stage, been sold for sizeable sums of money.'

CHAPTER SIXTEEN

SOMETHING
FISHY

The prosecution called mobile phone location expert Kevin Weeks. Under cross-examination by Lincoln's barrister, Mark Tomassi, Weeks confirmed that a mobile phone linked to Lincoln was in East India Dock, near the new Billingsgate Fish Market, at 4.40 on the morning of 3 April.

'Friday, 3 April is Good Friday,' said Mr Tomassi. 'You can take it from me that a lot of fish, I suggest, is sold on Good Friday. The timing is critical – this is the time of the alleged events. One of the men alleged to be part of the conspiracy, if all this data is right, is at Billingsgate Fish Market during the currency of what is believed to be the largest burglary in history. He buys fish and he goes home.'

Later that day, the phone was located near Lincoln's home. However, prosecutor Philip Evans said records showed his phone was later picked up in the vicinity of Hatton Garden and the home of alleged co-conspirator, John Collins. His car was also spotted in the London Bridge area, it was claimed.

According to phone records, Lincoln was next in contact with the group on Sunday, 5 April, once they had successfully gained entry to the vault, the court was told.

'Having agreed to be a party to the conspiracy, Lincoln agreed that his role would be as a getaway driver for the stolen property,' Mr Evans explained.

At the beginning of the second week of the trial, the jury was shown some more CCTV footage. This showed the unidentified thief known as 'Basil' strolling down Greville Street, which runs across Hatton Garden, with a black bag on his shoulder. It was then thought that he used a set of keys to get into the building. Later, Daniel Jones and another man turned up. They waited outside the building until Basil let them in through the fire escape. The prosecution claimed that the two men had been dropped off by the gang's white Transit van.

The prosecution called Detective Constable Jamie Day, who was the first Flying Squad officer to reach the burgled building on 7 April. He told the jury that the only CCTV camera working in the seven-storey building belonged to the independent company, Premises 21, on the second floor. Detective Constable Day said that a unit operating many of the cameras had been removed.

Mr Evans began questioning DC Day about Basil.

'It appears that he entered 88–90 through the main door, through the glass doors behind, through the lobby, past the lift on his right-hand side, through the door to the basement, down the stairs and into the area which is the corridor outside Hatton Garden Safe Deposit. And then through the door to the courtyard, up the iron staircase and through that little courtyard area to the fire exit door; the door to the fire exit is opened from the inside.'

Asked how this was done, DC Day replied: 'Simply the hand bolt – no keys required.' He added that from the outside, keys were needed if the door was locked otherwise it could just be pushed open. Soon after Basil opened the fire escape, other men entered the building, carrying tools and other equipment, and pushing wheelie bins, giving the impression that they were workmen involved in some maintenance job.

Under cross-examination, DC Day said that burglars took large amounts of jewels, gold bullion and cash, but boxes containing sentimental pieces or personal effects were ignored. A number of military medals were also left behind.

'A tape was found,' said barrister Nicholas Corsellis, representing Carl Wood. 'Ordinarily one might think that's something of very little value. It is a tape that related to a person, whose name is blacked out, admitting to something.'

A photograph of a black-and-silver Dictaphone that was in one of the boxes was also shown to the court.

Jurors were also shown pictures of the insides of Hatton Garden Safe Deposit, with lift shaft, with its damaged gate and door, and what they were told was an 'exact replica' of the 25 by 45cm hole the raiders drilled through the vault wall with a Hilti DD350 diamond-tipped drill. This was made from polystyrene from measures made by a specialist team using lasers.

Detective Constable Matthew Hollands told Woolwich Crown Court that the travel card found in Reader's wallet was used to travel from his home in Dartford to Hatton Garden on 2 April.

'It's an Oyster card,' he said. 'Freedom Pass.'

This is the pass allowing the over-sixties free travel on public transport in London.

Was Reader's name on it? the detective was asked.

'It is not, no,' said DC Hollands. 'It is in the name of a Mr T.

McCarthy. It does not have Brian Reader's photo on it, but it was found in his wallet.'

The court was then told that the burglars twice left a side door open, but Lionel Wiffen failed to grasp the significance of this and thwart the burglary. He had left at 9.21 p.m. on the Friday, just before Basil let the burglars in, but returned on Saturday to find the door ajar.

Asked if he was concerned about this, he said: 'Very much so. It has never, ever been open.'

He took a look around but saw nothing suspicious.

Mr Wiffen returned the following day – at 8 p.m. on Easter Sunday, midway through the burglary – to find the door ajar again. The elderly jeweller, who had worked at 88–90 Hatton Garden for thirty years, told Woolwich Crown Court he was 'nervous', but still did not realise that anything was untoward.

'I thought I would go to the caretaker and find out who he had given the key to,' he explained. He knew nothing of the burglary until it was discovered by security guards on Tuesday, 7 April.

Mr Wiffen also told the court he had felt uneasy for months leading up to the heist.

'There were cars parked outside the door on the other side of the road with people in them and they seemed to look over every time you opened the door,' he said. 'I was a bit nervous, to be honest. It seemed to be quite often – all different vehicles.'

The court was told that the security guard despatched to investigate when the burglars tripped the alarm was told to stand down as a previous alert had been caused by an insect. The alarm automatically sent a text message to the owners, who said that the burglars must have had 'significant information' about the security features of the vault.

Questioned by Mr Corsellis, security guard Kelvin Stockwell

agreed that the burglars would have needed 'detailed inside information' to pull off the job.

'I do not in any way seek to discredit you or cast any aspersions towards you, you do understand,' said Mr Corsellis. 'But it is plain to you, is it not, having worked there for as many years as you have, appreciating the complexities of the security system, where things are located, how things were bypassed, what area of the vault was drilled into, that the people who were involved in this crime must have had detailed inside information to commit this crime? Do you agree?'

Stockwell nodded. He then told the court that he had received a call in the early hours of 3 April, just hours after the alleged break-in began, from Alok Bavishi, son of the building's owner, to say the alarm had been tripped. As far as he was aware the seven-year-old system had not been triggered before, he said.

'He said the alarm system was sounding and going, he said the police were attending,' Mr Stockwell told the court.

The guard agreed to go and check the building. Arriving at around 12.40 a.m., he found no police on scene.

'I saw a couple, a young boy and his girlfriend, that's all I saw,' he said. 'I went to the front of the building and pushed against the front doors, they were secure. I went around into Greville Street to check the fire exit and I looked through the letterbox.'

Nothing caused the security guard concern so he returned to the building's front doors, he told the court.

'I called Alok, he said he was about five minutes away in the car,' said Stockwell. 'I told him the place was secure, he said, "Go home."'

In a statement read out to the court Mr Bavishi said he had received a call from a monitoring company to say the alarm had been triggered and the police alerted: 'They told me that the intruder alarm had been triggered and police were on the scene . . . I'm aware that this happened a few years ago and it was caused by an insect or similar.'

After setting off to check on the building, he received word from Mr Stockwell that the building was secure and thought it 'likely to be a false alarm'. Meanwhile, the burglars were hard at work under his feet until 8 a.m. that morning.

The break-in was not discovered until three days later, when staff returned from the Easter weekend. When Stockwell arrived at 8 a.m., another security guard, Keefa Kamara, was already in the ransacked building.

'He said, "We've been burgled,"' Stockwell told the court. 'I looked and there was a lock on the door and that had been popped. There was a hole through the wall and I saw that we had been burgled. On the floor there was drills, cutting material, the lights were on and the second floor [lift] barriers were left open.'

He also found a note had been left on the lift, saying it was 'out of order'. It was not there when he locked up the previous Thursday, he said.

'I went into the yard to get a signal and dialled 999,' Stockwell added.

The police arrived on the scene 15 to 20 minutes later, he told the court.

Hatton Garden Safe Deposit was protected by more than one alarm system. The building itself was fitted with an intruder alarm that was monitored remotely by a security firm, the court was told. Stockwell said anyone who triggered the alarm would have around a minute to key in the code, cancelling it into a control panel in the basement.

SOMETHING FISHY

The jury was shown photographs of the alarm system's keypad, which had been ripped off and the transmitter removed. The cover to the control unit had also been removed to expose circuitry and wires inside, and a grey power cable leading to the unit had been cut.

Stockwell said the basement and vault were covered by a second alarm system, which sounded and flashed lights. But he added: 'You wouldn't hear it from the street.'

Alok Bavishi's brother, Manish, told the court his theory was the burglars had knowledge of the design of the vault, which was installed in the 1940s, and of the basement, since they had not changed much since then. The family had owned the Hatton Garden Safe Deposit for around seven years. While they had improved the alarm system after taking over the premises, the codes had not been changed, he told the court. Two firms were used to supply and maintain an alarm system installed soon after the family took over. They would send contractors to service the system, he said.

The court heard that the lift had not been used to the basement level of the building, where the vault had been situated for more than thirty years, after an intruder armed with a shotgun attempted to break in.

The company policy was that, in the event of the alarm being triggered, security guards would go to the building, but were not to enter without the police being present. Mr Bavishi said he had provided police with the records of all his employees since his father took over running the vault, seven years before. He told the court that he did not know how to open the vault door himself and it was only the security guards who knew the combination.

The family were not based in London but live in the Sudan,

where he was at the time of the burglary, he told the court. He added that the heist had left the company insolvent and it had gone into liquidation. Mr Corsellis said he made no criticism of the family or the business for the huge losses suffered by their clients.

The trial progressed and on 8 December, the court heard from John Jeffrey, an antique jewellery dealer for over thirty-five years. For the last eight years, he had rented box 79 at Hatton Garden Safe Deposit. He told the court that, among other things, his box had contained £30,000 in cash, a diamond and pearl necklace, Georgian miniatures, low-grade gold bars and low-grade 'gold blobs', weighing between 100 and 300 grams, made from melting down scrap gold. These had all been taken during the heist.

Jurors were told that he visited his box once a month and he explained the process of accessing it. First, he had to be buzzed in by two separate guards and then two keys were used to open the box. Some 85 per cent of the contents had been there since he first rented it; the other 15 per cent was 'working stock'. He told the court items including an aquamarine antique brooch, an amethyst and gold brooch, and an emerald ring found at Perkins's house in Sterling Road, Enfield, belonged to him.

Mr Jeffrey explained how it had taken him three to four hours to look through photograph albums of the loot recovered by the police. He said it would have taken him even longer had he not been able to rule out the albums containing images of diamonds and wristwatches as he did not deal with those items. He said he recognised between thirty and fifty items, and another thirty pieces from photos of items grouped together.

'Six or seven albums had nothing to do with me,' he said. 'A lot of my items are so identifiable to me, it literally takes a couple of seconds.'

SOMETHING FISHY

After the raid, Mr Jeffrey had given police a list of things that he believed were missing. On the list was a navy-blue money bag full of 'scrap' – gold pieces that would be of greater value when melted down.

Asked about the sovereigns found at Harbinson's address, Mr Jeffrey said they were exactly the kind of things he would have kept in his scrap bag. Although he admitted there was no way for him to identify them as his, he said: 'If this was jewellery in your house, you wouldn't be popping the sovereigns out of the rings. This is how, when you are preparing to scrap something, you take it apart.'

Under cross-examination by Philip Sinclair, defending Harbinson, Mr Jeffrey was asked: 'If all of this had been found in my mother's jewellery box, you wouldn't be saying, "That is my scrap jewellery," would you?'

'No, absolutely not,' Mr Jeffrey replied.

On 9 December, the jury were given a little more information on the background of the masterminds of the heist when prosecutor Philip Stott read out a series of 'agreed facts' covering the criminal histories of the four men who had already pleaded guilty. Brian Reader, at seventy-six the oldest man involved in the robbery, was convicted for the Brink's-Mat gold bullion armed robbery in 1983. The gold was worth £500 million at today's prices. He was jailed for eight years for conspiracy to handle stolen goods, assisting in disposing of the gold bullion after the £26-million raid on a warehouse at Heathrow Airport; he was also convicted of dishonestly handling £66,000 in cash and sentenced to an extra year of imprisonment. Since his release and until recently, he had been living in a sprawling house in Dartford worth an estimated £1 million.

Sixty-seven-year-old Terrence Perkins was jailed for twenty-two years in 1983 for the armed robbery of the vaults of Security Express in Shoreditch. Like the Hatton Garden raid, this particular raid took place on an Easter weekend. It was masterminded by John Knight, brother of Ronnie Knight, the former husband of the actress Barbara Windsor. The gang netted nearly £6 million, making it the biggest cash raid in British history, and Perkins was subject to a £10,000 restitution order. He escaped from prison and spent fifteeen years on the run before being recaptured. Ronnie Knight later admitted handling some of the stolen loot and was jailed in 1994.

Seventy-five-year-old John 'Kenny' Collins also had convictions for offences including breaking and entering, theft and handling stolen goods, dating back to 1961. In 1975, he was given an eighteen-month prison sentence, suspended for two years, at Middlesex Crown Court for handling stolen goods. Then, in 1978, he was convicted of conspiracy to defraud the Post Office and one count of conspiracy to issue forged documents.

Sixty-year-old Daniel Jones had served sentences for robbery, burglary and handling stolen goods dating back to 1975. Many of his sentences were suspended, but he was jailed for five years in 1982 at Snaresbrook Crown Court for stealing jewellery worth £92,000 from Ratner's. Just two years earlier, he had been given a one-year sentence, suspended for two years, the same court for a £80 theft from a butcher's shop.

The jury was shown pictures of the interior of Jones's home in Park Avenue, Enfield, North London, which was described as 'opulent' and was owned by his partner, Valerie Hart. Mr Corsellis, defending Wood, described the premises as: 'A house of significant proportion, populated with items of considerable expense.'

Speaking of Jones, Mr Corsellis added: 'He's a man who wears his criminal heart on his sleeve.'

SOMETHING FISHY

While the court had previously been informed that around two-thirds of the haul, worth some £10 million, had not been recovered, Detective Constable Keith Jerham of the Flying Squad read out a statement indicating that the value of missing goods could be even higher.

'Based on the feedback from the victims, I am expecting the value of the property recovered, contained within a series of forensic photograph albums, to be in the region of £2 to £4 million,' he said.

CHAPTER SEVENTEEN

BARBECUED

The first defendant to take the stand was Carl Wood. He wore a beige V-neck sweater, white shirt open at the collar and dark trousers, and had his glasses on a cord around his neck. He was asked about his relationship with Daniel Jones, one of the ringleaders, who had already pleaded guilty to the burglary.

Wood said that they had met in a pub about thirty years ago and became friends because of a mutual interest in keeping fit. Soon afterwards Wood, then twenty-four, was diagnosed with Crohn's disease and had to cut down his physical activity. Instead, he and Jones would still go for walks together, often to a nearby garden centre.

'Danny is a very sensitive guy, a very funny man,' said Wood. 'Eccentric to extremes that everyone who knew Danny would say he was mad. He would go to bed in his mother's dressing gown with a fez on. He would read palms, tell people he could read their fortunes – bit of a Walter Mitty.'

Jones would talk to his white-haired terrier, Rocket, as if it were human. Then there was his obsession with crime.

'Danny was studying crime all the time in his room,' recalled Wood, 'reading books about it; watch films and go on the Internet.'

Jones was also crazy about the SAS and would doss down in a sleeping bag on the bedroom floor rather than go to bed; he slept next to his dog and peed in a bottle instead of going to the lavatory. At home he was also having running arguments with his wife, who was keeping on at him. The two men would often speak on the phone, but Wood explained this as 'general chit-chat' as they made arrangements to take a walk and nothing at all to do with crime.

The prosecution alleged that the phone calls actually involved plotting the Hatton Garden raid. Referring to a call made in early January, Nick Corsellis, Wood's barrister, asked: 'Were you discussing the planning of the largest burglary in English history?'

'No, I was not,' Wood replied. 'If I wasn't going on a walk, generally I was visiting my mum, with my wife or my children, or in the vicinity of my house. My life never changed other than that.'

Wood admitted that he knew that Jones was a career criminal, but they never discussed any criminal activities.

'He would tell me from time to time what he had been up to, but I never asked,' said Wood.

When asked why he did not use his phone – a cheap Tesco mobile – again after the burglary, Wood said he thought it had been stolen.

He told the court he was not 'Man F' on the CCTV footage as the prosecution alleged. Nor was he part of the gang involved in the burglary on the nights of 2 or 4 April: he was at home in bed with his wife when the vault was broken into. The following day, he was hosting a barbecue with his wife, daughter and grandchild. He did not tell the police this under legal advice.

A Barclaycard statement for Wood showed that he was £8,890 in debt earlier that year and his income was limited. He told the court that he supported his family on the £320 disability allowance received every fortnight because of his Crohn's disease and had only been able to work 'spasmodically'. He did not have a trade. However, he added: 'I do a bit of painting and decorating – just a general dogsbody.'

The disease was 'very painful and debilitating,' he admitted. Describing his condition, Wood said: 'It feels like a mouthful of ulcers with a bottle of vinegar in your mouth.' Nevertheless, the court was told, he rode a black motorcycle.

Wood had two grown-up daughters, Louise and Sophia. His mother was in a care home in nearby Ware, Hertfordshire, just eight miles from his home in Cheshunt.

'My mother has got Alzheimer's,' he said, as tears welled up in his eyes. 'She is bedridden, has been for four years.'

Referring to a series of phone calls exchanged between Jones and Wood, Mr Corsellis pressed his client: 'Do we understand that any communication you had with Mr Jones was either about exercise, gossip, chatting about sport, nothing of relevance?'

'Nothing whatsoever,' Wood replied.

Summing up the prosecution case, Mr Corsellis put it to Wood: 'You are in the loop, you are being updated by Mr Jones about this conspiracy. Is there any truth to that suggestion?'

'None whatsoever,' replied Wood.

When asked if he had any expertise in electronics, alarms or engineering, Wood said: 'No.'

It was pointed out that some of the calls that Wood received on his mobile phone from Jones were made shortly after Jones had also called Collins or Perkins. Wood told the jury that he did not know either man and had never met them.

He had little memory of his phone conversations with Jones. However, he did recall the details of a call he made on 28 March, less than a week before the burglary. He told the court that he had invited Jones to a barbecue at his house on Easter Saturday, which would have been while the heist was going on.

Wood also told the jury that Jones was having trouble at home.

'He said he was having murders at home, arguments,' said Wood. 'Val, his wife, was an agoraphobic, who was on quite a lot of pills for nerves. She would phone him all the time. He said he was in the middle of doing something important that involved a lot of money and "She is keeping on at me. She is on at me all the time. I have had enough, I can't take any more."'

Wood said that he cut the conversation short because he was not feeling well, but invited Jones to the barbecue because it sounded like he was going to leave his wife.

Referring to CCTV footage of the raid, Mr Corsellis asked his client: 'Are you Male F?'

'No,' Wood replied.

'Were you present as part of this burglary team on either the first night or the second night?' Mr Corsellis continued.

Wood replied: 'Full stop, I wasn't there at all.'

'Your defence is "It is not me, I wasn't there. I have an alibi – I was at home",' Mr Corsellis went on.

'Yes,' said Wood.

Wood said he spoke to Jones at around 8.30 a.m. on the morning of Saturday, 4 April. During the 50-second call, he again invited Jones over to the barbecue at his house, he said.

BARBECUED

He told the court: 'Danny phoned me in the morning to say that he would come to the barbecue. Is there anything he needed to bring, he said, and what time should he come? I said about lunchtime.'

Wood told the jury he had already stocked up on burgers, sausages and chicken from his local Tesco in Cheshunt. He then added that Jones later called him again, this time pulling out of the barbecue and urging Wood to 'keep watching the telly' as something was obviously up.

'He told me he was sorry he couldn't make the barbecue that teatime – I think I moaned a bit and I just wanted to get off the phone, really,' said Wood. 'He made a comment at the end – "Just keep watching the telly and you will see." I think he knew that I was annoyed that one minute he said he was going to the barbecue and then he wasn't.'

Mr Corsellis then asked: 'And when he gave his name as Mr Vinnie Jones perhaps he was giving a nod to a certain celebrity?'

This was, perhaps, a reference to the name Jones had given in Machine Mart in Twickenham, when he had bought the new pump.

'Sorry?' queried Wood.

'It doesn't matter, never mind,' said Mr Corsellis.

Wood admitted that he knew about Jones's criminal past. After the barbecue, he added, he went to bed and read a book.

Beginning his cross-examination, Mr Evans returned to the matter of Wood's financial situation. He owed some £23,000 in credit card debts and loans and was 'living on the breadline', the court was told, and 'didn't have two pennies to rub together'. The court was told that Wood owed almost £9,000 to Barclays, more than £3,000 to NatWest, up to £2,000 for a Christmas loan and almost £9,000 to a friend. Wood had phoned Barclaycard two days before the raid began, asking for advice about the money he owed. The day after the raid, he called debt advisers.

'Your debt situation, I suggest that was your motive for committing these offences,' said Mr Evans.

'No, it wasn't,' said Wood.

'On 7 April, your hopes that your problems were going to be cured by your profits from the Hatton Garden burglary raid had disappeared,' Mr Evans continued. 'That is why, on 7 April, the first working day back, you were on the phone to both of your most significant debtors . . . That is right, isn't it?'

'That is your suggestion,' Wood replied.

Mr Evans then directed the jury to the evidence of the police surveillance, where Jones and Perkins were recorded as saying someone called 'Carl' must be 'cursing himself' and considering suicide.

'That "Carl", that is you, isn't it?' he asked Wood.

'Where does it say that?' Wood replied.

Mr Evans then accused Wood of lying to the jury when he told them he was bad with numbers and could not remember his daughters' birthdays or when he got married.

'You are making up your evidence as you go along, aren't you?' said Mr Evans. 'You are lying to this jury, aren't you?'

Wood denied this.

Mr Evans referred back to the telephone conversation Wood had had with Jones, where Jones apologised for not coming to the barbecue and where Wood said Jones had told him: 'That thing I was talking about – just keep watching the telly.'

Wood said when news broke of the raid he suspected Jones's involvement as Jones had a previous criminal record, so he knew what he was capable of. And earlier, Jones had alluded to being involved in something to do with a 'lot of money'.

BARBECUED

Asked why there was no contact between himself and Jones after the raid, Wood said: 'I had semi-convinced myself Danny was involved and I didn't want to have anything to do with him, and I also assumed Danny was busy and didn't want to have any contact with me.'

Mr Evans showed him CCTV images from the basement of the safety deposit company of a man identified by prosecutors as 'Man F', seen wearing glasses similar to Wood's. Wood repeatedly denied it was him in the images.

'That man has glasses, lives in Cheshunt, is called Carl, is white, about the right height, and he knows Danny Jones, and is in regular contact with Mr Jones. It is you, isn't it?' said Mr Evans.

'I totally disagree. It is not me,' replied Wood.

Mr Evans then showed the court a picture of a white Transit.

'The person who is driving is Mr Jones and you are in the passenger seat,' said Mr Evans.

Wood denied it.

'You agreed with these men, you agreed with Mr Jones, maybe in a café or on a walk or on the telephone, you agreed to take part in the burglary at Hatton Garden,' Mr Evans said. 'You went on that first night and were part of drilling that hole.'

'You're wrong,' Wood replied.

'You went back the second night. You got spooked, didn't you?' Mr Evans asked.

'Never,' replied Wood.

Mr Evans also accused Wood of lying about his alibi for the Easter Saturday evening, the second night of the burglary, where he said he was at home with his wife and daughter, having a barbeque.

Wood denied he was lying.

'Not only did you take part in a burglary, the reason you were going to do it is because you're a man in a great deal of debt and you relied on this being the end of your problems,' said Mr Evans. 'It was all part of your agreement to burgle and conceal the proceeds. Your alibi is a lie. And you've now implicated your wife and daughter.'

Paula Wood, Wood's wife of nineteen years, was then called. Wood wiped tears from his eyes with a handkerchief when she told the jury that he had been at home in bed with her on the night of 4 April.

Asked where her husband was that evening, she said: 'He was with me. I cleaned up and pottered about and sat down for the evening and watched TV with Carl.'

Mrs Wood said she went to bed between 11 and 11.30 p.m. and slept next to her husband. They both slept in the same bed over the Easter weekend, she said.

When asked when Wood had last spent all night away from home, she said: 'Not for years, not since he was young, in his twenties.'

She added: 'He would have been at home with me. I would remember more if he hadn't been at home, but he would have been at home with me.'

Dressed in a pastel-green woollen sweater, Paula Wood told the court that she and her husband had hosted a barbecue at their home in Cheshunt on 4 April but it was a 'flop' after her daughter and Wood's friend Danny Jones had both pulled out.

Asked again by Wood's barrister, Mr Corsellis, where Wood was on 4 April, Paula Wood replied: 'I'm telling you, my husband was with me.'

For the prosecution Philip Stott then put it to Mrs Wood: 'The first time that the authorities – the prosecution, the police, the court – were told that you could vouch for your husband's whereabouts was in November this year.'

The court was then told that Mrs Wood was interviewed by police on 21 November, just days before the trial was due to open.

Mr Stott suggested that Mrs Wood would do anything for the husband she had known for forty years.

'What I suggest, Mrs Wood, regretfully, is that you have come to court, taken the oath and then lied about your husband's whereabouts on the night of Thursday, 2 April,' he said.

'I have not lied,' Mrs Wood replied.

'In respect of the Saturday night, I suggest to you that you have lied about there being a barbecue in the afternoon,' Mr Stott went on. 'What's being suggested is that you and your husband have got together and come up with this explanation, to this jury – on oath, lying to them, in order to try and protect him.'

'I cannot stand here and lie on the Bible,' she replied.

Asked how she felt when her husband was arrested on 19 May, Mrs Wood said she was 'shocked'.

'I thought my husband was coming back the next day, I really did. But I was in shock,' she admitted. 'It was a shock that something that . . . serious . . . accusing your husband of . . .'

The jury also heard evidence from Wood's younger daughter, Sophia, who said she had attended a barbecue with her son and parents at around 5 p.m. on 4 April. She also said that, as far as she knew, Jones was due to attend the event.

CHAPTER EIGHTEEN

BILLY THE FISH AND FAMILY

William Lincoln, who was accused of being a getaway driver, told the jury that he was at Billingsgate Market, buying fish with his friend, whom he knew only as 'Jimmy Two Baths', when the burglary took place. He went to the market every Friday to buy eels for his mother, who lived in Essex. Depending on what his friends and family asked him for, he would also buy Dover sole, cod, haddock or skate – hence his own nickname 'Billy the Fish'.

Lincoln claimed that he remembered being at the market at around 5 a.m. on 3 April. Data from his mobile phone shows he made a call to 'Jimmy Two Baths'. Earlier, he had promised to introduce his friend to the fishmonger's at the market so that he could buy his own seafood wholesale. Lincoln told jurors that he knew Jimmy from Porchester Hall steam baths in Westminster.

'He's called "Jimmy Two Baths" because he goes down twice,' explained Lincoln.

His barrister, Mark Tomassi, then asked Lincoln: 'Were you involved in the burglary at Hatton Garden Safe Deposit?'

'No, sir,' said Lincoln.

When asked if he was able to understand the charges against him, Lincoln said: 'I am not a divvo, but I am not the sharpest knife in the drawer.'

The court was told that Lincoln suffered from sleep apnoea, bladder problems and severe osteoarthritis, which led to him having a double-hip replacement. Due to these ailments, he was unable to work and received Disability Living Allowance and Employment and Support Allowance.

Lincoln broke down in tears as he recalled an incident with his grandson, who he said was the 'light of his life'. His daughter had asked him to look after the boy but he was unable to, and while under the care of someone else, the two-year-old boy had suffered a head injury. He was now in an induced coma in hospital.

After Lincoln said he blamed himself for the accident, Mr Tomassi asked: 'When people ask you to do things, what is your reaction?'

'I never refuse to do anything,' he replied.

Lincoln admitted looking after three bags for Collins.

Though he lived on benefits, Lincoln admitted leaving the country two days after the raid. He took a Ryanair flight to Rhodes before hopping on the ferry to the Greek island of Symi, where he spent fifteen days fishing with an old friend. He claimed he knew nothing of the Hatton Garden diamond heist, even though some of the missing jewellery was found at his home in Bethnal Green.

Although he was accused of dropping Reader off at London Bridge Station after the first night of the burglary, Lincoln said he had not seen Reader until they appeared together at Westminster Magistrates' Court, charged with burglary. He explained he had been that side of the river because, after he had finished at Billingsgate, he had gone to Borough Market to stock up on fruit and vegetables. Then he spent the rest of the weekend making preparations for his holiday, which had been booked some time before.

He told Woolwich Crown Court that he travelled to Gatwick Airport and flew out to Greece on the morning of Tuesday, 7 April. The night before he left, he had visited his sister's home in Bletsoe Walk, Islington, which she shared with Collins.

'When I went round there, I was talking to him,' Lincoln recalled. 'I bought some euros off him. While I was there, I noticed some bags . . . three bags. I probably went, "What, has she chucked you out?" when I saw them bags. He said he had sold his house – it was all old pictures, paperwork, some bric-a-brac . . . I believe it was his dad's house. He hadn't had any time to arrange any storage and then he asked me if I had anywhere I could store it, and I left with the bags. I took the bags home with me.'

Not long after Lincoln got home his nephew, Jon Harbinson, arrived for a cup of tea and a chat.

'As he was leaving, he saw the bags. He said, "How long are you going for?" I said, "No, that's not my gear, I'm looking after it. I have got to put it up in the loft."'

Lincoln said Harbinson offered to take it and put it in his shed. He did not see the bags again until the 19 May, when he took them from his nephew's taxi and put them in Collins's white Mercedes outside Doyle's plumbing workshop in the car park of the Old Wheatsheaf pub, Enfield. When Collins was arrested a few minutes later, the bags were found to contain large amounts of jewellery.

Lincoln's barrister, Mr Tomassi, asked: 'Did you, at any time, open and look at the contents of the three bags?'

'No, sir,' he replied.

He was arrested shortly after the exchange when officers boxed in his black Audi as he drove along the A10. Addressing the 'ladies and gentlemen' of the jury, Lincoln gave a colourful description of the event. It was 'pandemonium,' he said with 'swearing going on with both parties.

'I'm screaming "Ahhhh, my f***ing hips!"' he said, explaining he had a double-hip replacement.

Lincoln said he was forced face down onto the road, but when officers realised he had a weak bladder, they took to a grass verge to urinate. Later, he said he was humiliated at Wood Green police station, where he wet himself when officers did not take him to the toilet on time.

Lincoln also told the court he had been given a separate bag of jewellery by Collins on the day before he was arrested, to see if he could sell any of it.

'It was in a clear bag and he said, "Can you sell any of this?" I took a couple of rings,' Lincoln said. 'I left the rest of it in the airing cupboard and the bits I wanted, that I thought I could sell, I put behind the skirting board with a bright yellow duster.'

When police searched his home, officers had found a plastic bag containing jewellery wrapped in a yellow duster cloth behind the skirting board in his living room. They also found a bag of jewellery in an under-stairs cupboard, items of jewellery in a sock in the bottom drawer of a bedroom, and £2,000 in £50 notes under his microwave.

Lincoln said the money had been left to him by his brother, who had died in his arms – he had withdrawn it from his late brother's bank account at his request to give to people who had looked after him.

James Creighton, aka 'Jimmy Two Baths', took the stand and said that he and his friend 'Billy the Fish', aka Lincoln, used to 'do quite a lot of schmeissing' – the Yiddish for 'whipping'. Schmeissing is a speciality of the Porchester Baths. The technique is carried out in a hot steam room, where the body is soaped all over with a coarse brush and then scrubbed vigorously.

Harbinson then took the stand. He said that he had no reason to suspect that the three bags he was storing in his garage for his uncle were stuffed with jewellery from the Hatton Garden raid. He had first seen the bags in the corridor of Lincoln's Bethnal Green home when he had gone there to talk about his grandmother – Lincoln's mother – who was ill.

'I assumed it was his luggage he was taking on holiday,' Harbinson told the court. 'I asked how long he was going for because there was a couple of bags in the hallway. He said he had to put them upstairs, could I help him – in the loft, I think he said.'

Asked by his barrister, Philip Sinclair, what he was told was in the bags, Harbinson replied: 'He just said it was a load of old shit.'

Mr Sinclair then asked how they had ended up in his silver Mercedes Vito taxi. Harbinson replied that he couldn't remember exactly.

'It is a question I have been asking for the last seven months,' he said.

He left the bags in the vehicle overnight before putting them in his garage the next day before going to work.

Harbinson said he did not think anything further about the matter until 18 May, when Lincoln arranged a meeting the following day in the car park of the Old Wheatsheaf Pub in Enfield. He then became suspicious as the bags were taken out of the side door of his people-carrier taxi and put into the boot of someone else's car.

'What did you think was going on?' asked Mr Sinclair.

'I didn't have a clue, to be honest,' said Harbinson, 'but it wasn't right.'

Afterwards, he deleted the address of the car park from his satnav.

He admitted being ashamed and embarrassed that he had stored bags containing stolen jewellery and had moved them in his taxi.

'People are saying that I knew,' he said. 'That I picked up stolen property – that didn't do.'

He said he now felt stupid and naïve for trusting his uncle, who had asked him to store the bags. At one point, Harbinson was asked why, after he had answered some questions at the police station after his arrest, he had then stopped answering.

'Honestly,' he said, 'because the solicitor kicked me under the table.'

Harbinson said that he had been estranged from his uncle for twenty years and they had only been reconciled for the last year. He had not spoken to his aunt for ten years either.

'It's a bit of a pattern with me,' he told the court. 'I fall out with people.'

When asked about items of gold jewellery hidden under the cupboards in his kitchen, Harbinson said one piece, a necklace, was given to him by his grandmother. He told the court it had sentimental value to him. A sovereign ring was a present from his parents, while the half-sovereign was a gift from his sister when he got his first job. The gold chain he had bought for himself. He said he had also bought the two Cartier watches that were found by detectives.

Harbinson was then shown a police surveillance photo taken almost a month after the heist, showing three of the ringleaders who had pleaded guilty, talking in an Islington pub. He said he did not know two of them, although of course he did know Collins, the man in the middle, who lived with his aunt, Millie Garrett.

Cross-examining, prosecutor Philip Stott asked about the copy of *Killer* found in Harbinson's home in Beresford Gardens. Stott alleged that a page in the memoir detailing a theft using high-powered drills 'exactly like Hatton Garden' was marked with a piece of grey card.

Harbinson told the court that when 'I was told about the book, I had no knowledge of it.'

In *Killer*, Charlie Seiga, once billed as the 'Houdini of the criminal Underworld', described robbing the vaults in sorting offices, where high-value parcels and cash were kept. The haul would be between £200,000 and £400,000.

'Like everything else, with the advancement of science things improve and progress, and now we too had progressed,' wrote Seiga. 'We were using more advanced methods. Instead of the primitive way of blowing a safe we were now using diamond drilling equipment to open up these impenetrable safes and vaults.'

The paperback was published in June 2002, years before the Hatton Garden job was planned.

Seiga's gang used a drill with a 10-inch diamond bit, like the one used in the Hatton Garden heist. Seiga also listed the rest of the equipment needed to drill into a vault. This included another high-powered drill to mount the bolts attaching the main drill to the wall, a transformer weighing some 5 kilograms, an extension lead and a water hose at least 100 foot long. This would be attached to a water pump. Water had to be fed to the cutter to keep it cool and speed up the cutting, Seiga explained. It also kept the noise down a bit. Then there were crowbars for gaining entry and ripping alarm bells off the walls and hacksaws for cutting phone cables, screwdrivers, spare fuses and other back-up equipment, all of which 'cost quite a few bob, but they were our working tools and were essential'.

Seiga then explained how the job was done. First, the electricity supply had to be located, then the wires would be cut.

'We would all sit off the place with our scanners on for a good hour or so, listening and watching,' he wrote. 'After this was done we would go and put the alarm bells out of action and sit off for another hour and, if it was all OK, we would then go in with our tools.'

Seiga's gang would always work at weekends, going in Saturday evening and coming out early Sunday morning. It could have been a blueprint for the Hatton Garden job, only picking a bank holiday weekend, they went one better.

Referring to Seiga's book, Mr Stott said: 'He is talking about his criminal life and heists he had been involved in. Is that something you had an interest in?'

'Many years ago, possibly,' Harbinson admitted.

'There was a bookmark in this page,' said Stott.

'That's what you say, but I don't know, I wasn't there,' said Harbinson.

'Were you interested in the plan you were engaged in?' asked Stott.

'I wasn't engaged in it,' said Harbinson. 'If this book is so prevalent in evidence against me, why wasn't it forensically examined?'

'It was bookmarked on a page that is exactly what took place in Hatton Garden,' said Stott.

'I had no knowledge of what happened in Hatton Garden,' Harbinson insisted.

Stott then showed him the grey card found in the book. Harbinson agreed it was probably the back of a book of taxi receipts.

'This was your book and you were reading it, weren't you?' Stott persisted.

'No, sir,' said Harbinson, denying the book was his.

The jury was then shown the CCTV of the handover in the pub car park. Mr Stott suggested to Harbinson that he knew exactly where the contents of the bags came from.

'The only way that they knew you could be trusted not to call the police or steal from them was because you were Lincoln's family,' the prosecutor suggested.

'You are asking me to answer a question about what other people think,' said Harbinson.

'You were family, you wouldn't inform the police and you were paid,' Mr Stott continued.

'I was never paid,' Harbinson replied.

'You were going to be paid to ensure your silence . . .'

'I was never offered any money and I never received any money,' Harbinson insisted.

'. . . and to try to reduce the risk of you stealing out of the bags,' Mr Stott continued.

'That is not true,' said Harbinson. 'Everything you have said about me is not true.'

Harbinson had never been arrested before the Hatton Garden raid.

'I don't steal from anyone,' he insisted. 'None of my friends think I am a thief or a dishonest man.'

He also maintained that in the series of calls between himself and Lincoln in the weeks before the Hatton Garden raid, they were discussing the deteriorating health of his eighty-two-year-old grandmother. The court heard evidence that she suffered from chronic kidney disease and renal failure and her condition deteriorated in March.

The trial was adjourned over the Christmas period and would resume on 4 January.

CHAPTER NINETEEN

CLOSING
THE CASE

During the trial, a gold necklace was designed celebrating the heist. The pendant was shaped like the three overlapping holes the burglars had bored through the vault wall. Produced in 18-carat gold, the necklace was made by one of the local jewellers and costs £570.

East London designer Joe Bruce, who worked in advertising, said that he decided to create a lasting tribute to the burglars. He told the *Evening Standard* that he hoped the piece captured the audacious spirit of the heist.

'Like many people who regularly pass through Hatton Garden, I became fascinated by the heist,' he explained. 'The hole they cut in the wall has become a bit of a symbol for the audacity and brutal simplicity of the raid. There was a lot of cheekiness about it and that's what I tried to capture. I'm not celebrating the crime, I'm picking something interesting about the case and cementing it.'

THE GREAT DIAMOND HEIST

The design was called 'Hatton Tom Foolery' and was originally intended as a present for his wife. He approached several jewellers in Hatton Garden with his design.

'Most of them were nervous about getting involved,' admitted Bruce. 'But the one who agreed is one of the best in the area and he loved it.'

Nevertheless the craftsman concerned preferred to remain anonymous, but has now put the design into production. Each piece takes two to three weeks to make. Bruce said he was not seeking to make a profit and the £570 price tag only covered his costs.

Another memorial was mooted. David Pearl, property mogul and vice-president of Tottenham Hotspur football club, announced in December 2015 that he was considering opening a museum on the site of the jewellery heist. His property company, Structadene, bought the leasehold to 88–90 Hatton Garden when it was put up for sale on behalf of the liquidators. The leasehold, asking price £200,000, plus £230 a year, lasts until 2033 and includes the offices, showrooms and the vaults.

Pearl told the *Evening Standard*: 'There could be a museum around the incident, it could be revamped to have high-security and new deposit boxes, or let to a jewellery shop.'

*

The Christmas recess also gave various authors and intellectuals ample opportunity to riff on the more esoteric aspects of the case. The American news website the *Daily Beast* looked into the reasons the whole world was entranced by big burglaries like the Hatton Garden heist and concluded: 'It's because we dream of skeleton keys that will unlock the hidden parts of our urban lives.'

CLOSING THE CASE

The *Beast* said:

> Billed as the 'biggest burglary in English legal history', the April 2015 Hatton Garden heist in central London is already the stuff of legend – from the silver-haired suspects and their *Ocean's Eleven*-style intricacies to the loot discovered in a graveyard. Within moments of the crime's revelation by a stunned Metropolitan Police, media outlets outdid one another to produce architectural diagrams of the targeted building, down to the black silhouettes of unidentified men shown abseiling down empty elevator shafts and cutting holes through solid concrete walls. One reporter for the BBC even taught himself basic climbing skills and familiarised himself with a specific make of concrete drill in order to re-enact the heist – for useful forensic insights or merely for clicks, it was hard to say.

The *Beast*'s reporter Geoff Manaugh went on to point out that what was known about the heist came largely from the police recordings using hidden cameras in the Castle pub, indicating the criminals' stupidity in meeting there and openly gloating over their spoils. On the other hand, they had been clever enough to use a diamond-tipped Hilti DD350.

'Hilti tools are already known for their combination of raw power and sonic discretion,' Manaugh wrote. 'Recent tests in New York City have favoured a municipal shift to Hilti tools for use in public construction projects precisely because they produce less noise. They are a late sleeper's – not to mention a bank robber's – best friend.'

Geoff Manaugh is also the author of *A Burglar's Guide to*

the City and commented on the prevalence of hi-tech tools in modern-day larceny. 'What are commonly thought of as "burglar's tools" – such as lock picks, crowbars, and bump keys – are far surpassed in both efficiency and function by the official tools of breaking and entering used by maintenance crews, SWAT teams, and fire departments,' he said.

Equipment already existed that gave almost unlimited entry into even the most secure buildings, though usually public access to these tools was carefully regulated. Mostly, they required such detailed training that the list of criminal suspects was limited to a number of qualified operators and, when a concrete drill like the one used by the Hatton Garden gang was found at the scene, the trail would lead an investigator back to the construction industry. Indeed, the Metropolitan Police soon traced the Dad Army's drill to a theft at a nearby building site.

When details of the drill appeared in the media, Google hits on the Hilti website spiked and Manaugh suspected that others were dreaming that they were 'just one extension cord away from secret treasure'.

Manaugh was also intrigued by Joe Bruce's design of the pendant in the shape of the hole the robbers had drilled.

'The idea that a bank heist could produce a geometric symbol so recognisable as to become iconic reveals something about the imaginative hold a crime like this can hold over a city,' he said.

Other writers commented on the 'subterranean pull' of London.

'The epidermis of the city is so heavily policed,' author and filmmaker Iain Sinclair wrote in the *London Review of Books*, 'so fretted with random chatter, so evidently corrupted by a political assault on locality, that humans unable or unwilling to engage in a war they can't win respond by venturing into forbidden depths.'

CLOSING THE CASE

There was a fad for billionaire homeowners to construct mega-basements, while lone eccentrics William Lyttle, aka 'the Mole Man of Hackney', in the course of forty years from the 1960s on, built such an extensive network of tunnels under his East London home that he undermined the foundations and the pavement outside collapsed. There are numerous books and websites about abandoned tube stations and underground rivers. All over London manhole covers and mysterious trapdoors lead to subterranean shafts and passages. Even Labour leader Jeremy Corbyn got in on the act, admitting to Lorraine Kelly on ITV's *Daybreak* that he was a drain-spotter and collected manhole covers.

In the 2008 film *The Bank Job*, the fictionalised version of the 1971 Baker Street raid, the heist succeeded due to the accidental discovery of a medieval plague pit that extended up to the bank's foundations.

*

When the court reconvened after the Christmas holidays, Harbinson's partner of twenty-two years and mother of his three children, Cherie Wright, was called next. She said there was nothing unusual about his behaviour at the time of the robbery and that family photographs taken more than ten years previously showed him wearing some of the items the police had found stashed at the house. Detectives had even found photos taken of Harbinson with his daughter some fifteen years earlier, which showed him wearing one of the watches the police had found, she claimed.

She insisted she was '100 per cent sure' that a ring seized in the search belonged to her partner; the couple also owned the other items. The valuables were hidden around the house because he was 'a little bit security-conscious'.

'I told them [the police] he has had them for years and they are insured,' she said.

She told the court that she did not go into the garage or see the holdalls. She also said that the book *Killer* had lain untouched in a cupboard for six years. It had been given to Harbinson by a friend ten years earlier and was inside a box that had not been opened for years. She had never seen him reading it.

When the heist had taken place, she told the jury that she and her two eldest daughters had been at a pony show. But she had seen Harbinson over the course of the weekend and said she had noticed nothing strange about his behaviour. He had gone to see his uncle because he was worried about his elderly grandmother.

Prosecutor Philip Stott accused her of concocting a fake story as she had told police at the time that she did not recognise the jewellery.

'The fact is you have changed your evidence,' he said. 'You initially said you didn't recognise them, because you didn't recognise them. You said that because you had no idea where they had come from, and you have now made up this story, having spoken to your husband about the best thing to say.'

Doyle's defence counsel Paul Keleher QC then told the jury the events of 19 May, when the prosecution alleged some items from the Hatton Garden jewel heist transferred in the car park near Doyle's office were 'absolutely nothing to do with him'. Indeed, his presence was a problem for the others.

'They were actually momentarily put off their stroke by the fact that Mr Doyle was there,' Mr Keleher explained. 'They did not expect him to be there, but once they ascertained he was leaving, they carried on.'

He said his office was in a former sheep shed at the back of the Old Wheatsheaf pub, off Chase Green. His partner leased the building directly from Punch Breweries, rather than the pub landlord, he added.

'It was part of the actual lease agreement that we have no claim to any parking spaces in the car park,' he explained.

Doyle told the jury that parking had been 'a big bone of contention'. When the building was renovated under the lease agreement, the pub landlord 'was not happy about parking'. He had known Collins, who ran his own pawn business, for some fifteen to eighteen years and had met him at the Old Wheatsheaf in May because he was going to lend him one of his vans. Collins, who used to import fireworks, also wanted to store fireworks in the loft above his office.

'He was the kind of guy that would buy expensive watches and buy it off you and sell it back to you when you had the money, almost like Cash Converters,' Doyle explained. 'He was selling his father's old property and was going to clear it out and borrow one of my vans to do that. His health had deteriorated – he had diabetes and was going deafer every time I met him. I thought he had retired.'

Doyle told the court that Collins also 'said he was owed money from fireworks and he was thinking about taking goods to their value, and was looking to store them somewhere, and goods from his father's house. He basically needed the storage.'

Doyle said he had arranged to show Collins the loft space on 18 May – the day before the loot was exchanged – but he did not have the right ladder with him that day and suggested that he came back the following day. However, he 'started going a bit cooler on the idea' of storing fireworks there when he saw that the shed was being used as an office.

'He thought it was storage, but it's not – it's coming together as an office,' Doyle explained.

He had given Collins a key so he could let himself in and make coffee when he returned the following afternoon.

'I had no idea what they were planning,' Doyle said. 'No idea at all.'

In the CCTV footage of the handover, Doyle was seen touching Danny Jones on the arm in a familiar fashion, although he claimed it was the first time he had ever met him.

Under cross-examination, he told the court he used to drink with three of the admitted ringleaders – Collins, Perkins and Reader – about once a month for a year or two in the late 1990s or early 2000s, although it was only Collins that he considered to be a friend. He said he found his drinking companions amusing and was aware they had a criminal past, but he did not know the specifics because 'people in that line of work tended to keep quiet'.

'You knew, because of those meetings, that Brian Reader and Terry Perkins were men that had involved themselves in crime?' asked Mr Evans for the prosecution.

'I didn't know any specifics about their past,' Doyle replied.

'You say you didn't know specifically, but you knew that Mr Reader and Mr Perkins were two men involved, in their past, in serious crime?' Mr Evans continued.

'I didn't know it was anything about serious crime,' said Doyle.

'What did you talk about on these twenty occasions, what were the general topics of conversation?' asked Mr Evans, pressing him.

'It was fifteen years ago, so I can't remember any specifics, but they were just funny,' Doyle replied.

He went on to describe Collins as 'a real Arthur Daley character' and insisted he was friends with him, but the others were mere acquaintances.

Mr Evans then pressed Doyle on the CCTV, in which he can be seen tapping another ringleader, Jones, on the arm.

'That morning, on 19 May, was the first time you'd met Daniel Jones?' Mr Evans asked.

'First time ever,' Doyle insisted.

He denied making up an excuse to get a colleague and his wife, Jenny Fraser, out of the office so the men could use the premises. However, he had been taped by the police telling Collins he would 'get rid' of an employee by telling him to fetch a coffee. Doyle explained that he wanted to show Collins his office and did not want to put an employee who might not be part of the plans into an embarrassing situation. He denied accepting any payment from the known robbers.

'There was no agreement entered into,' he said. 'I had no knowledge of what was taking place. The car park is a public space. Never in a million years would it be a good place to do something stupid like that.'

'That's why you gave him the key,' Mr Evans said.

Mr Evans accused Doyle of lying to the jury and pointed out that in court was the first time he had mentioned anything about the arrangement with the key.

'I am telling the truth,' Doyle insisted. 'That was dead space for me – if you could use that space to subsidise the rent for the business, it's just good business.'

Doyle later complained he had had only 'very limited access' to a solicitor due to tight security arrangements at the time the defence case was being prepared.

'Is there anything you've thought of which is inaccurate about this defence case statement?' Mr Evans asked.

'I can't think of anything,' Doyle replied.

Doyle's wife, Jenny Fraser, testified about plans to pick up her mother at 10 a.m. on the day of his arrest in May. She said her husband asked her to come into the office first to sort out problems with the phone lines and agreed that CCTV footage showed she had left there at 9.50 a.m. She had not seen Doyle meeting the other three men outside, and he did not mention it to her later.

At the time, Ms Fraser said: 'I think I was on the phone, I was on my computer.'

She said Doyle had not told her to leave, saying: 'I would have been late to go to my mum's house to pick her up for her birthday.'

She did not know that Doyle had given a key to Collins. Later, the padlock had been changed to a combination lock to avoid the inconvenience caused by the loss of keys. But this change took place after May, she said.

After Ms Fraser's evidence, Judge Kinch QC told the jurors the evidence in the case had been brought to a conclusion and they would move on to the summing up.

CHAPTER TWENTY

A MATTER OF
TRUST

In his closing speech to the jury, Philip Evans QC said that the defendants had lied to the jury when they denied their involvement in the Easter weekend robbery. They had, he said, cooked up their story during their time in prison together since their arrest and they were the trusted accomplices of the men who had already pleaded guilty.

'Ask yourself this question: If I had gone to all the trouble of burgling the safety deposit boxes at Hatton Garden, would I be likely to let out of my sight someone I didn't overwhelmingly trust with millions' worth of jewellery and diamonds?' he said to the jury. 'Just take a step back, because it has become a bit like Groundhog Day, coming to Woolwich in the morning, going back at night – losing a little bit of sight of what this is actually about. What we are talking about is £10 million worth of jewellery to £14 million worth of jewellery. That is a staggering sum of money. I imagine many of us would be extremely excited if we were to win the lottery to the tune of £14 million. That is what we are dealing with.'

He went on to deal with the victims of what otherwise seemed like a victimless crime.

'The property belonged to people who have no doubt worked hard to run their businesses, to get that property together and keep their businesses going,' Mr Evans added.

He then asked the jury to consider whether the ringleaders would have trusted those on trial to look after the loot and not take a peek inside the bags they had been given.

'Do you really think for one moment that Mr Collins is just going to say on the off chance that Mr Lincoln doesn't have a quick glance inside the bags?' asked Mr Evans. '"Some bags of old shit" – that is how Mr Lincoln describes those bags, as he thought they were. Do you believe that for one second?'

He pointed out that the raid was so carefully planned that at one stage it was thought to have been an inside job. It was clear that those involved knew what they were doing and knew where the safe deposit boxes were, where the alarms were, and where the CCTV cameras were, Mr Evans told the jury.

When it came to the defendants' evidence, he said: 'In this case, lies have come from the defendants from that [witness] box. On each of the four occasions that you have heard the defendants give evidence, each of them has told you lies. Some of them might have been half-truths. But in the end, the evidence which you have heard is not true.'

Mr Evans told the jurors that the accused had been able to put their heads together while inside Belmarsh Prison and decided on a story that they would all stick to.

'The men who have pleaded guilty were a group who thrived, didn't they, thrived on acquisitive crime – taking people's money and possessions, greed in reality,' he said. 'What they needed were people who wouldn't question them. People like Carl Wood, who used to go on all of his walks with Dan Jones, who told you time and time and time again we chatted about "bloke's things".'

Wood knew that Jones had been questioned about an incident in Bond Street, and suggested he was aware of his criminal background. The court heard that Wood was chosen because of his connection with Jones, with whom he would go on regular walks and whom he knew was a 'crook'.

'He could trust him not to open his mouth and tell the police that Dan Jones was planning something big,' continued Mr Evans.

Despite their detailed knowledge of the building's layout and alarm system, the criminals overlooked a single camera at the back of the building.

'What they forgot, or didn't know, was that one little camera in that walkway outside the back of the jeweller's was still working and recording what they were doing,' said Mr Evans. 'And from that you were able to see them going in and going out, and you were able to see what they took with them.'

Mr Evans also highlighted that in his evidence Doyle admitted knowing Reader, Perkins and Collins, and often going drinking with them in a pub near Hatton Garden.

'They were never going to let that significant commodity go into the hands of someone they did not trust,' he added.

Mr Evans again insisted the four men had not told the truth to the court.

'On each of the four occasions that you have heard the defendants give evidence, each of them have told you lies,' he said.

He added that it did not matter what size role each of the men had played because 'if you take part knowingly, you're guilty'.

Then it was the defence's turn. Nicholas Corsellis, defending Carl Wood, said that the Hatton Garden robbery could be turned into a Hollywood movie but Wood did not fit the script.

'This is one of the reasons Mr Wood is not guilty. What did he bring to the table?' he said. 'He would have only been able to act as a general dogsbody. He called it illogical and implausible that such a person was involved as criminals are not charitable people.

'This case has given you a glimpse of the inside track to serious organised crime. This is an important aspect of Mr Wood's defence. The reason is, that the way that this crime was planned and effected demonstrates Mr Wood's innocence,' insisted Mr Corsellis. 'Criminals who are going to take part in this exercise do so for one reason only: money, and hopefully lots of it. It's not about improving your reputation, publicity or Instagram following. It's not about doing a person down on his luck a favour, it's all about the money.'

Anyone involved in the burglary must have had the necessary skills to be able to assist on the nights in question. The gang were serious organised criminals who had put a team together, where each member has to have a role – an alarm man, an electrician; a lift engineer.

'And what would they have said about Mr Wood on such an analysis?' he asked. '"We need someone to touch up the paint when we leave?"'

He added that an inside man must have been involved.

'We suggest the team must have had someone who had been inside the vault before and who knew where the possible pitfalls were,' Mr Corsellis said. 'The redundant lift shaft, the CCTV in the caretaker's room, the telephone box in the cleaner's room, the particular fuse box in the boiler room… That someone also knew what could be safely left. For example, the JCS CCTV – that was a dummy camera and was not targeted, and that the disguises were perfect for the Berganza camera.'

He continued: 'As Mr Evans said, there will be times in the future when this case will be referred to in public – on the radio, in a book, or on TV.

'Well, since the prosecution have raised the topic it would be wrong of me not to address it . . . more likely on the big screen. You can imagine the film titles – *Bad Grandpas* or *The Enfield Expendables*? The comedy is clearly there. And if so, who would play Carl Wood? You can imagine the film agent's task. Who can we get to play Carl Wood – The Extra Pair of Hands? Do you think Mr Tom Hardy or Mr Vinnie Jones is going to rush to take the part of the EPH?

'It doesn't fit the script, does it? Unrealistic, because an EPH is illogical, implausible, unrealistic . . . It makes no sense as there was an EPH, because Male F was actually a player. An inside man, or linked to the inside man – fully familiar with the inner workings of Hatton Garden Safety Deposit Ltd.'

Mark Tomassi, defending Lincoln, said that Collins was described as 'wombat thick' by his accomplices. Recorded conversations between Perkins and Jones show that Collins was terrified and wanted out.

'Mr Collins was so scared, so petrified, that he would have given it to anyone. He had lost the plot and he wanted rid of it,' explained Mr Tomassi. 'You may think it would be unfortunate to infer the reason he gave it to Mr Lincoln was that Mr Lincoln was trusted by him. There is no evidence that he has opened the bags, inspected the contents, or physically touched anything inside.'

According to him, Lincoln simply handed them on to Harbinson, who stashed them in his garage. There was no evidence that Harbinson had looked in the bags either.

On Wednesday, 13 January, the jury retired to consider its verdict after hearing seven weeks of evidence. The judge instructed the jurors to seek a unanimous verdict in each case.

The following day, the jury returned with its verdict. Wood and Lincoln were found guilty of conspiracy to commit burglary and conspiracy to conceal, convert or transfer criminal property. Doyle was convicted of concealing, converting or transferring criminal property. Harbinson was cleared of all charges. The convicted men showed no reaction when the verdict was read out.

While Wood and Lincoln were to remain in jail, Doyle was allowed out on bail again. Judge Kinch said: 'He has been convicted, albeit of the slightest of counts on the indictment of any defendant in this case. Nonetheless, his conviction [is] in relation to involvement in an extremely significant matter, and one which is likely to carry or result in a custodial sentence. That said, I take the view that he has acted responsibly since being granted bail.'

It was then the turn of the pundits to discuss why the thieves had failed to pull off what everyone conceded was a brilliant plan. Age, all agreed, had something to do with it: they were simply too out-of-date to implement their plan without being caught. Consequently, it was doomed to fail.

They were tripped up by new technology they did not fully understand, making the elementary mistake of using their own phones instead of throwaway 'burner' phones. The gaps in their movements were filled in using records from the network of ANPR cameras around London, so it was relatively easy to see where the men had been during the weeks before and after the burglary.

Others would learn from their mistakes and avoid such an old-fashioned caper. Former Scotland Yard commander Peter Spindler, who oversaw the investigation, said: 'It's probably the last of its type.'

He added that the gang had made a string of errors that meant it took the police just a fortnight to identify them as prime suspects.

'They probably thought they had got away with it, and became complacent or arrogant,' he went on. 'They were analogue criminals ill-prepared for digital detectives. That's how they got caught. They are men of their time, one of the reasons they have not been successful – a decade or two ago, there was not the ANPR or CCTV coverage there is now, and they would have had a better chance of getting away with it.'

Nor was it a victimless crime. Of the forty box owners to be identified, many were jewellery traders like Sammy Akiva, who was uninsured and lost hundreds of thousands of pounds.

'The police told me, "Your box has been broken" and honestly, I didn't know where I was,' he said. 'I was screaming. I took it terrible.'

Mr Akiva said he continued to suffer ill health from the shock of the burglary, felt dizzy all the time and was on medication.

Baljit Ubhey, the chief Crown prosecutor for London, said that although £4 million had been recovered, every effort would be made to find the missing £10 million.

'There absolutely will be ongoing investigations to uncover more of the property and so I don't think the defendants should think they've got away with the other two-thirds,' she said. 'If prosecutors can show the burglars tried to convert their property, the CPS can go after their assets. We can apply for restraint, we can apply for confiscation, and that doesn't matter if that happens years later.'

CHAPTER TWENTY-ONE

BAD DAD'S ARMY

The media were quick to piece together how the Hatton Garden heist had been pulled off and how the aged outlaws had got away with it, perhaps so that everyone would forget just how wrong they had got it at the time. Meanwhile, the BBC was ready with *Bad Dad's Army: The Hatton Garden Heist*, which contradicted almost everything said in their *Britain's Biggest Diamond Heist? The Inside Story*, nine months earlier.

Airing just a day after the verdict had been handed down, the BBC had the head of the Flying Squad, Detective Superintendent Craig Turner, saying: 'I was quite surprised. They were obviously elderly, but they were career criminals. And it was certainly my impression that it was one last graft for them to take. It was, in fact, their pension pot.'

Barry Phillips, whose punditry had been all over the newspapers in the days following the raid, was there too.

'The lure was too good,' he said. 'The greed was there. They probably thought they were invincible. An arrogance kicked in and they were given an opportunity for one last hurrah.'

Criminologist Professor Dick Hobbs was called on to give academic insight.

'I think you can compare it to old boxers,' he said. 'They retire, but they get an offer to go back in the ring one more time for a big prize. And this was a big prize.'

DC Jamie Day, the , the first Flying Squad officer to arrive on the scene of the burglary, was called on to vouchsafe a few thoughts on Brian Reader.

'He has been described as the governor, the master, the organiser,' he said. 'He would see himself as the top of the tree in his group. He is a career criminal. He has previous convictions, notably for being involved in the Brink's-Mat robbery.'

This was key to his thinking, according to criminal psychologist Dr Donna Youngs.

'Reader's involvement in the Brink's-Mat theft was an indication of the same sort of desire to carry out the big dramatic crime that gets him remembered,' she said.

According to Barry Phillips, Reader was the kingpin. He had the skills needed to pull off a criminal enterprise and the contacts in the criminal underworld to put a team together. First, he would have recruited Kenny Collins to recce Hatton Garden and check out the premises. Collins was also the lookout and the all-important getaway driver. He was a man with sufficient form to be trusted.

At sixty, Danny Jones was the baby of the group. He was brought in as the muscles and was key to getting into the vault. Sixty-seven-year-old Terry Perkins was the fixer, who took on responsibility for the drilling. Then there was the mystery man, 'Basil', who seems to have been an engineer sent in to disable the alarms. The name 'Basil' was picked up from police bugging operations. Otherwise nothing else was known about him.

Everyone seemed to love that the old-timers planned the raid over pints in the Castle pub in Islington. However, it is unlikely that they spread blueprints of the vault out on the bar room table, as depicted in the BBC documentary.

The heist was not just about the money they were going to get away with, said Phillips: 'They are also looking towards laying down the bragging rights within the criminal fraternity by committing and getting away with Britain's biggest heist.'

Former bank robber Bobby Cummines concurred with this view.

'What will give them the greatest notoriety but respect in the criminal underworld is that it is a crime without violence,' he said. 'It's a little bit of a boast that you've had Hatton Garden over. They could have stuck up a jeweller's shop, but to do Hatton Garden, that's a little bit special.'

The BBC had a bit of black-and-white newsreel footage, showing the new-fangled strongroom being opened in the 1940s. The police do not yet know where Basil got the key, but at 9.22 p.m., he got into the building at 88–90. Then he opened the fire escape and let the others in.

The gang then sent the lift up to the second floor and disabled the sensor so that the doors would not close and the lift could not move. They left a handwritten 'Out of order' sign in case it was discovered.

With the lift stuck on the second floor, they were able to get into the lift shaft, with a clear drop straight down into the basement. It is thought that Jones and Basil scrambled down as they were the fittest. Despite earlier news reports and the antics of the BBC's Declan Lawn, they did not abseil.

At the bottom, they jemmied open the gateway and then attempted to disable the intruder alarm by cutting through a telephone cable and snapping off the back-up transmitter's aerial. They cut the power cable to a magnetic lock on an iron gate and smashed through a wooden door, letting in the rest of the gang, who hadn't come down the lift shaft. Using an angle-grinder, they cut through a second metal gate to reach the vault door.

But the drillers were not experts, as had been thought: the pensioners had picked up their only skills by watching clips on YouTube. The alarm had not been triggered deliberately, as 'Razor' Smith had suggested. They were unaware that the alarm they thought they had deactivated had sent a text-message alert and the security guard was on his way. But they got lucky when the police failed to grade the alarm properly and decided not to respond. Otherwise the security guard would have opened up the vault and they would have been caught in the act.

However, their good fortune proved short-lived. When they drilled through the reinforced concrete wall of the vault, they hit the back of the cabinet housing the safety deposit boxes. It was bolted to the ceiling and the floor, and they were unable to shift it. After almost eleven hours' work, they gave up and left empty-handed at around 8 a.m.

The situation became a true test of character. After years of planning, Reader found he could not handle the setback and decided to withdraw. Barry Phillips speculated that he had seen the writing on the wall. Bobby Cummines put it more succinctly: 'At the time, it's good when you are planning it, but when you have had a pop and it ain't worked, then you reflect – the game has gone out of it and you are looking at the reality of it. That's a different ball game. And if people looked at the reality of it, they would never do it in the first place.'

Nevertheless, the others rose to the challenge. Having got within millimetres of the prize, they found it impossible to walk away.

Of course, returning to the scene of the crime was a huge risk. They waited for a day and a half. There was no coverage of the attempted robbery in the media. It seemed the aborted raid lay undiscovered and the lure of the diamonds was now irresistible.

Even though these men were hardened criminals, they had to psyche themselves up again. When they found the fire-escape door locked, Wood could not hold his nerve and left. But Basil still had his key to the front door and they entered as before.

This time they brought with them a new hydraulic ram. With it, they were able to dislodge the metal cabinet blocking the hole they had drilled. But the hole was small and the aged thieves had grown portly. It is thought that only Jones and Basil entered the vault. Even then, it would have been a tight squeeze.

Once inside, they began forcing open safe deposit boxes and passing the contents out through the hole in the wall.

According to Bobby Cummines: 'Once you are in there, it is like a kid at Christmas, opening up presents. They just are just popping boxes and inside the boxes, it's all prizes.'

Professor Hobbs found it puzzling that the men had opened so few boxes, given the amount of time they were in there.

'The deposit boxes are not hard to break into, once you are actually in the vault,' he explained. 'I don't know whether they felt they had had enough, enough money, enough loot, or whether they were targeting certain boxes. It's interesting.'

Packing the gold, gems, jewellery and cash into bags and wheelie bins, they trundled it up the stairs, leaving via the fire escape. Loading over £14 million worth of loot into their white van, they made off without getting caught. It was by far the biggest payday of their careers and these old-time crooks thought they had got away with it. Another two days went by before the theft was finally discovered and they must have thought they were in the clear.

When the Flying Squad heard that there had been a burglary in Hatton Garden, they decided it was one for them. Formed in 1919, they took their name from the fact that their jurisdiction knew no boundaries. They were the one of the first to use cars and their insignia was a swooping eagle.

The Flying Squad broke the Great Train Robbery, Brink's-Mat, the Dome robbery and Graff.

DSI Turner, head of the Flying Squad, said: 'The people we recruit onto the Flying Squad are thief-takers. They can get that evidence together to successfully prosecute people that go to court.'

'There has not been a major robbery that has not been solved by the Flying Squad,' added Barry Phillips.

Having failed to answer the alarm, the Met's reputation was on the line and the traders who had lost millions put on the pressure. For the Flying Squad, it was a race against time: could they catch the gang before they got rid of their haul? All the early speculation was that a gang that could pull off a heist of this size and ambition would have the right connections to get rid of the loot.

Fortunately, the streets around Hatton Garden are full of cameras that capture images of everything that moves – including the white van bringing the crooks to the raid. Examining the CCTV footage, the Flying Squad quickly realised that the gang had been through twice. It was clear that something had gone wrong on the first attempt. No matter how well planned the heist had been, the gang would not have thought through what they were going to do in this eventuality and they would start taking risks.

On the second night, they made the mistake of checking out the building in Collins's Mercedes. A Mercedes E200, it was highly distinctive and there are very few of them on the road; white with a black roof and black wheels, even with the grainy CCTV footage it was easy to track the car.

Once the Flying Squad had Collins under surveillance, he quickly led them to other members of the gang. Covert officers watched as he and Perkins met for their regular Friday night drink in the Castle to explain to Reader what had happened when they went back.

Detectives also planted electronic listening bugs in two cars used by the gang – Collins's Mercedes and Perkins's blue Citroën Saxo – and overheard the crooks bragging about what they had done, unaware that the police were listening to every word. They had been on the biggest robbery in the world; nothing like it would ever happen again. Although they were quite surprised to have pulled it off, they were convinced that they had got away with it scot-free.

In the recordings from his Citroën, Perkins was heard to boast to Jones: 'That is the biggest robbery that could have ever been. That will never happen again. The biggest robbery in the world, Dan.'

The pair discussed hiding part of their haul from other members of the gang in Jones's in-laws' graves.

Jones said of the smaller of the two packets: 'We'll say that, that's our bit.'

However, they were also suspicious that others were holding out on them.

Perkins said: 'You wouldn't know if someone's took a stone out of these parcels.'

'You'd never know in a million years,' Jones replied.

They had heard on the news that a 12-carat diamond had been stolen.

'I ain't seen it,' said Perkins.

'No, f*** me!' replied Jones.

The recordings of these conversations proved a goldmine of evidence for the police. They now knew exactly who the ringleaders were and how they had pulled off the heist. What's more, it was clear the robbers still had the stolen property since they had not yet divided it up.

The scale of the heist was causing them problems. It would be difficult to launder it and turn everything into cash, so it could be split up. Some of the older criminals had made their reputations as men who could shift stolen goods; they had decades of experience. But at some point it would have to be moved, and an exchange made.

The Flying Squad had to play a waiting game. According to the press, the police were at sea with the investigation and the heat began to die down. Around six weeks after the heist, Collins's distinctive Mercedes was caught on CCTV at a pub car park in Enfield. He was seen scouting the area with his dog, Dempsey. Then he met his old friend, Hugh Doyle, who ran a business next door to the car park.

It was clear to the surveillance officers that Doyle's yard was the perfect place to transfer some of the loot. If they did a boot-to-boot exchange in the street, it would look like a drugs deal to any passing police officer or member of the public. They did not want to lose everything they had worked for during the last three years over a simple error like that: the car park area gave them some degree of privacy. But they did not realise that it was within shot of a security camera, nor did they know they were being tailed by the Flying Squad.

The following day, 19 May, the CCTV caught Collins arriving in his Merc. Jones then turned up on foot. Lincoln arrived with his nephew, Jon Harbinson. Three bags were taken from Harbinson's taxi and stowed in Collins's Mercedes.

According to DC Day: 'The three bags that had been exchanged behind the pub contained at this point an estimated £2 to 4 million worth of diamonds and gold.'

The exchange done, Collins and Jones drove off with a boot full of loot in the same distinctive Mercedes Collins had driven to Hatton Garden on the second night of the heist, the beginning of the gang's undoing. With the Flying Squad on their tail, they drove to Perkins's daughter's house nearby – she was away.

The police now had everything they needed. They had pictures of the principal gang members meeting up and the recordings of them saying what they had done. Now was the chance to catch all three of them with some of the stolen property. There was no reason to delay the arrests any longer, so they decided to go in.

The Flying Squad swooped, nicking Collins, Jones and Perkins with the three holdalls from the car-park exchange. These contained millions of pounds worth of loot. A search of Collins's house revealed a large amount of cash, watches, jewellery and a money counter. At Jones's property, police found facemasks, a drill and some cash, while at Perkins's home, they discovered jewellery, cash, blue overalls and white gloves.

Hundreds of officers stormed twelve addresses in London and Kent. It was important that the rest of the gang should be arrested immediately, before they had a chance to dispose of the remainder of the loot and disappear altogether. As it was, it was surprising just how much of the loot was still in their homes.

'Given the professionalism and the care that the crime had actually been carried out with, it's a bit surprising that there wasn't more professionalism in the moving of the goods afterwards,' noted Professor Hobbs.

The aged larcenists were surprised by their arrests and obviously very disappointed. They had thought they had got away with it. Collins, Jones and Perkins realised what trouble they were in when they saw Brian Reader in the same police station. But they were experienced criminals and remained poker-faced, giving no indication that they knew one another.

In their minds, they would have been working out how to minimise their criminal responsibility. But then they were interviewed and detectives took them through all the evidence they had amassed against them. Once they realised how comprehensive the investigation had been against them, it must have been clear that there was no way out. Nevertheless, they dug their heels in and answered each question with a deadpan: 'No comment'.

Collins, Jones and Perkins were played their bugged conversations, while Reader was shown photographs of himself with the others. For them, the game was up and they duly confessed to their crimes. Lincoln, Wood, Doyle and Harbinson continued to maintain their innocence, though. After their six-week trial, Lincoln, Wood and Doyle were convicted, while Harbinson alone was found not guilty.

The maximum sentence for the crime was ten years. With their guilty plea and time spent on remand, the ringleaders could be freed after three years. But because two-thirds of the loot was still missing, the men faced further action under the

Proceeds of Crime Act, punishable by a maximum of ten years without remission.

On 21 March 2016 the Crown Prosecution released details of the sentences. Of the four who initially pleaded guilty to one count of conspiracy to commit burglary, Collins, Jones and Perkins were each sentenced to seven years' imprisonment, while Reader received six years and three months. The judge said that he had taken into account that Reader was 'seriously unwell' following a stroke he suffered while being held at Belmarsh Prison. He also suffered from prostate cancer and loss of hearing, and needed assistance to carry out simple tasks. Indeed, Reader had been unable to come to a hearing on 6 March because he had been rushed to hospital suffering from septicaemia. He is likely to die in jail.

Of those found guilty after trial, Lincoln was sentenced to seven years in jail for conspiracy to commit burglary and seven years (to run concurrently) for conspiracy to conceal, convert or transfer criminal property; for the same offences Wood was sentenced to six years in jail for each (to run concurrently). Doyle, who was found guilty of concealing, converting or transferring criminal property, received twenty-one months' imprisonment suspended for two years.

Terri Robinson and Brenn Walters both pleaded guilty to one count of concealing, converting or transferring criminal property, for which they were each sentenced to eighteen months' imprisonment suspended for two years.

CHAPTER TWENTY-TWO

THE HOLE-IN-THE-WALL GANG

Although some details of the gang members' criminal pasts had been given in court, the worst aspects had been suppressed to prevent the jury being unduly prejudiced and the trial being compromised, but it turned out that the men who committed the Hatton Garden diamond heist were not the cuddly bunch of old-fashioned crooks they were made out to be, but violent thugs who would stop at nothing to get away with the loot they needed to fund their lavish lifestyles.

Brian Reader grew up in the bombed-out streets of wartime South-East London and worked as a butcher's boy before following his spiv dad Henry into the criminal underworld. But Henry Reader was a small-time crook – his son turned out to be anything but that.

Reader's rap sheet begins in 1950, when the eleven-year-old was found guilty of breaking into five shops. He was given a twelve-month conditional discharge. Over the next twenty years, he turned his hand to what would become his specialities – burglary and handling stolen property – and by the late 1960s he was working with a group of Britain's top thieves. They were behind dozens of major burglaries and robberies, clearing out warehouses and jewellery workshops – often around Hatton Garden – and netting millions of pounds. It was said that he was good at disposing of stolen property and had contacts for getting rid of stolen jewellery among Hatton Garden's less scrupulous dealers.

Reader is alleged to have led a gang dubbed the 'Millionaire Moles', who tunnelled 40 feet into the vault of Lloyds Bank in Baker Street in 1971 and escaped with a £3-million haul, worth £41 million today. Three of the men were arrested and eventually jailed, but only £250,000 of the proceeds was recovered.

According to *The Independent*, the Baker Street raid had been organised by five members of the group but only one of those was convicted – Tony Gavin, who was sentenced to twelve years. The other two men convicted only had minor roles in the raid. Along with mastermind Reader, there was Gavin's usual partner-in-crime, Mickey 'Skinny' Gervaise, a burglar alarm expert, and another associate known as 'Little Legs' – a common nickname at the time for short men. The fourth of the insiders who escaped arrest was a 'shady character' dubbed 'TH', who was connected to Scotland Yard Detective Inspector Alec Eist.

Under a cloud for allegations of multiple corruption, Eist was returned to uniform in 1976, monitoring parking wardens. He was acquitted in an unrelated corruption trial after his retirement in 1977 and died some years later. According to documents obtained by *The Independent* from the late 1970s corruption inquiry into the Met, 'Operation Countryman', Eist was suspected of receiving jewellery stolen in the Baker Street raid.

Reader took the precaution of spending his time abroad. According to *The Times*, criminal intelligence linked him to a £1 million robbery at Heathrow in 1977.

In 1980, Gervaise was arrested, turned Queen's Evidence and became a 'supergrass'. Among those he named were Reader, Gavin, Eist and 'Little Legs', who swiftly left the country.

Reader's lawyer said that his client vehemently denied being on the Baker Street raid: 'This is clearly speculation and hearsay – and you will note that my client has never been arrested or questioned by the police regarding the incident, nor has he been subject to any investigation by them.'

Reader was also said to have broken into a vault in Holborn Circus in 1982 – while on the run after earlier raids – and got away with £1 million in jewels, worth £10 million today. He avoided capture by spending time abroad and once took his wife Lynne on a luxury weekend to Paris to ensure he had an alibi for a job being planned by another gang.

In April 1982, he faced trial for £1.3 million stolen in burglaries in Hatton Garden and Birmingham. But the trial collapsed when a juror reported a bribery attempt. Rather than face a second trial, Reader skipped bail, hiding out in Spain and France.

While on the run with his family overseas, he sailed yachts around the world and took winter holidays in French actress Brigitte Bardot's favourite Alpine resort of Méribel, where his children learnt to ski. Reader, it was said, loved the finer things in life – holidays, good wine and food, especially Italian. Those were the days before European arrest warrants.

However, his wife Lynne later told the crime journalist Duncan Campbell for his book *That Was Business, This Is Personal*: 'I hated it. I thought – you can't go home when you want to. People think it sounds glamorous, but it was awful.'

They eventually returned home when her mother fell ill.

Next came the £26-million Brink's-Mat robbery. This was no old-fashioned smash-and-grab raid. Security guards were doused with petrol and threatened with lighted matches until they agreed to open the safe. Having set out to steal a mere £3 million in cash, the thieves stumbled on 10 tonnes of gold bullion, then had the problem of disposing of it.

Senior figures in the criminal fraternity were called to help – for a cut. The Adams family were happy to oblige and employed the services of jeweller Solly Nahome, who was willing to sell on the smelted-down gold. Some twenty murders have been associated with the Brink's-Mat heist.

John 'Goldfinger' Palmer was another involved, though he was acquitted in 1987 of knowingly handling gold from Brink's-Mat. Then there was Kenneth Noye, recruited, with Reader, to sell the gold once it had been smelted.

Reader was said to have been with Noye when he stabbed DC Fordham. Noye was acquitted of murder on the grounds of self-defence, while Reader claimed that he was not present at the time. However, bruising on Fordham's arms indicated that he was being held when he was stabbed. According to *The Guardian*, Reader also aimed a kick at him.

A police source told the *Daily Mirror* that they believed Reader had nothing to do with the killing.

'Him and Noye were like chalk and cheese,' the source said. 'Reader is the last of the gentleman thieves. He was a likeable bloke, not arrogant or aggressive like many villains. He didn't have the swagger or the bravado of people like Noye.'

Reader got nine years for handling gold from the Brinks-Mat robbery. He was cleared of the earlier robberies after a supergrass withdrew his evidence against them, but jailed for two years and fined £2,000 after admitting contempt of court by absconding. Terry Adams, who stood trial alongside them on the gold handling charge, was acquitted. Much of the stolen bullion was never found.

Reader was still associated with Noye in 2000 when he used his son's phone to call him. This led to his capture.

'Reader never sussed it was his boy's phone being used by him that put Noye on the radar,' a source told *The Sun*. 'He thought he could pull the same stunt while putting the Hatton Garden job together.'

According to the source, Reader planned the Hatton Garden raid because he couldn't resist the buzz of one last job, though some say he was out to get at some of the missing Brink's-Mat gold stored in the safe deposit boxes. It was thought that he started planning as early as 2006, when he recruited Basil, an alarm breaker also known as 'The Ghost'. He dreamt of smashing open the 1940s-built safes hidden deep in the vaults of the Hatton Garden, believed to contain up to £200 million in bullion, cash and gems.

It became a possibility in 2010 when he got a key to the front door from a bent jeweller. The original plan had been to drill through the door of the vault with help from a safe engineer the gang had befriended but he was not a dedicated criminal and backed out. Then Jones came up with the idea of drilling through the wall.

After Reader decided not to return on the second night, Perkins and Jones were determined not to give him a penny from the job. Wood, too, was left empty-handed, while Basil received a fraction of his fair share.

'Perkins, Collins and Jones said, "We're taking that," and Basil hardly had anything,' a source told the *Daily Mirror*. 'I warned him not to get involved with those three. The biggest diamond went missing and it turned up in Collins's pocket.'

Meanwhile, Reader continued to demand his share.

'That old c*** still argues. He knows he ain't getting a dollar,' Perkins was overheard saying.

'He knows it now,' said Jones. 'If he doesn't, he's a c***. He's still hanging on, though, ain't he? He knows he ain't got no friends no more.'

The good times were well and truly over for Reader and his family. Following his guilty plea, they were ordered not to sell their home while the authorities decided whether to confiscate it. Despite his reputation as a quiet family man, few will pity Reader. A career criminal who knew the risks, he lived the high life on the back of his crimes for half a century. Now he is likely to die in jail: his defence counsel, James Scobie QC, believes that he 'does not have many months to live'.

Terry Perkins was branded 'ruthless and evil' as he was jailed for twenty-two years in 1985 for his part in the huge Security Express robbery. He turned thirty-five on the day of the robbery and celebrated his sixty-seventh birthday on the Hatton Garden heist.

Gregory Counsell, one of the security guards at Security Express, said that Perkins and the other Security Express robbers warned him they had kidnapped his wife and daughter, and threatened to blow his 'f***ing balls off' with a shotgun.

'People may think they are modern-day Robin Hoods but that is far from the truth,' he declared. 'They were ruthless criminals and they were going to kill me. They are horrible people.'

Collins had convictions for robbery dating back to 1961 and was most recently jailed for nine years for a £300,000 armed jewellery raid in 1989. Released on licence in 1993, he was plainly past his best. On lookout again on the second night of the Hatton Garden heist, he nodded off and had to be woken by Basil. And Jones has convictions for robbery and burglary dating back to 1975. Choosing a sleeping bag on the floor over getting into bed with his agoraphobic wife, Valerie, he was obsessed with the army and jogging and claimed to have supernatural powers.

Although diagnosed with Crohn's disease, an inflammatory bowel condition, in his early twenties, which he claimed often left him bed-ridden in agony, Hackney-born Carl Wood also had a long criminal record. A suspected cannabis dealer, he stood trial in 1993 with two police officers, who had teamed up with crook Robert Kean in a bid to recover £600,000 owed to the villain by an underworld financier. They were caught by police corruption busters, who secretly filmed them at a hotel where Wood was heard bragging that he would beat the debtor with an iron bar after claiming he also owed him £80,000. After torturing the underworld money launderer, he would dump his body in the sea. He was jailed for four years for his role in the plot.

In conversations recorded by police bugs, Perkins suggests Wood was vouched for by his old friend Billy Hickson, who stood trial alongside Perkins for the Security Express heist.

Wood was around £20,000 in debt, but in January 2015 attended the Adventure Travel Show at Olympia Exhibition Centre in Kensington. This offered 'once-in-a-lifetime travel experiences'. Clearly he was anticipating future wealth.

He did not attend the planning meetings for the Hatton Garden heist, but was regularly updated by his friend of thirty years, Daniel Jones. The pair would regularly meet for walks, followed by sandwiches and coffee at their local gardening centre.

Although he denied taking part in the heist, the jury believed that he was the figure dressed in dark clothing, hi-visibility waistcoat and navy baseball cap and wearing a white surgeon's-style mask, dark gloves and glasses seen entering 88–90 Hatton Garden on the first night of the raid.

Lincoln was recruited by Collins as a trusted family member who would control a large part of the loot after the heist. He had a string of convictions for attempted burglary, burglary and attempted theft between 1975 and 1985, but his most recent conviction was for battery in 2013. A tough East Ender, he attacked a gang of youths with a chair because they were causing trouble on the street outside his home in Bethnal Green.

The married father-of-two was known as 'Billy the Fish' for his connections with Billingsgate Fish Market and would regularly turn up at the Porchester Spa with salmon to sell to his fellow bathers. However, with a double-hip replacement and a bladder problem that had left him incontinent, he lived off disability benefits. He was not fit enough to be part of the team that went into the building and was arrested after organising the handover of the loot.

Hugh Doyle was another of Collins's trusted friends. Born in Ireland, he moved to the UK when he was seventeen. With his partner of twenty years, he set up a plumbing business called Associated Response from their home in Enfield in 2009.

In 2014, they took over the lease of a converted sheep shed from Punch Breweries to use as an office. The brewery company also owned the Wheatsheaf pub, which shared a car park with his business premises.

Doyle was not party to the planning of the burglary and never went to Hatton Garden. However, he was contacted by Collins (whom he had known since the late 1990s) when he needed a place to hand over the stolen loot. He gave Collins a key to the padlock that secured the wooden doors of the small brick-built shed but instead they carried out the handover in the pub car park, in full view of CCTV cameras.

Doyle was arrested, along with the gang's ringleaders, on 19 May. He was charged with conspiracy to burgle and remanded in Belmarsh Prison's most secure unit, alongside Britain's most dangerous criminals and terrorists, and denied visits from his family for three-and-a-half months.

Having spent most of his time behind bars exercising, Doyle lost two stone. He also got hold of a copy of Christopher Hitchens' book *God Is Not Great* so he could counter the religious arguments of the extremists on his wing.

When the burglary charge was dropped just a week before the trial was due to start, Doyle was granted bail, fitted with an electronic tag and restricted to a 9 p.m. to 6 a.m. curfew. He went back to work and would do plumbing jobs before and after the court day, arriving in his company van and wearing his work uniform in the dock.

Friendly and talkative, Doyle knew the court staff and reporters covering the case by name, even offering his professional services to some journalists, who took his phone number.

Barry Phillips said: 'This firm were not cuddly old men – they were professional villains, some with a history steeped in violent crime.'

But underworld legend Fred Foreman, who teamed up with Perkins on the Security Express robbery, insisted: 'These old boys should be applauded for what they did. They weren't ponces scrounging benefits and wanted to do one last job to look after their families. They showed true British bulldog spirit and deserve absolute respect.'

Former enforcer for the Kray Twins, eighty-three-year-old Foreman added: 'I would love to have been on that job. It was their last hurrah. They are family men, who wanted a pension and to give the missus and kids a few bob. I hope the judge goes easy on them.'

Despite this display of British virtue and family values, clearly what was missing from the Hatton Garden diamond heist was some love interest. However, *The Sun* was happy to supply this. The day after the gang were convicted, they came up with a gangster's moll, who helped nail the 'Diamond Wheezers'. She was said to have had a relationship with a gang member and grassed him up in revenge for jilting her.

'There is a lot of head-scratching going on because they know there is always an informant on a job of this kind and the police were onto them too quickly,' a source told *The Sun*. 'The strong suspicion is that a woman known to one of the team was upset with him for some reason and bubbled him up.'

Another source added that police were onto the gang within a day or two, which they also believe is due to information given by a woman upset with one of them, but described the truth as 'a jealously guarded secret'.

During the case, it was revealed that in bugged conversation Perkins was heard talking about a woman called 'Randy Mandy' and another woman like her.

'See that bird there,' he told Jones, 'Randy Mandy is a bit better than her, but like her.'

But there was no suggestion that it was 'Randy Mandy' who had grassed up the gang. Nor has it been confirmed if there are any links between the woman and the arrest of the gang.

CHAPTER TWENTY-THREE

THE ONE THAT GOT AWAY

After a year, the police still had no idea who the eighth man, 'Basil', was. This was particularly embarrassing as he was the insider, the key player who let the robbers into the building. And he may have got away with most of the loot.

In CCTV footage, he appeared to be tall and slim, and to have red hair, although he may have been wearing a wig. A bag he carried on his shoulder obscured his face. Scotland Yard admitted they hadn't a clue and renewed their offer of a £20,000 reward for information leading to his arrest and prosecution. The file was also been forwarded to Interpol and Europol.

DSI Turner said: 'The Flying Squad has a reputation for getting their man and we won't give up.'

They should have looked no further than the *Daily Mirror*, who said that Basil was a computer genius headhunted by Reader after the elderly burglar witnessed his nerves of steel when overcoming the most sophisticated security systems.

While he was known as Basil in the court, after that name was overheard in bugged conversations, it was probably not his real name. To the underworld, he was known as 'The Ghost'. Most of the gang had no idea of his true identity. Only Reader knew who he was and even he did not have his phone number.

But the *Mirror* underworld informant seemed to know almost everything about him.

'He's a clever kid and the police won't have much on him, he's too good for that,' the source insisted. 'He will have hidden his whack somewhere secure in the UK and gone on his toes. I don't know where he is now. On every job you need a good alarm man and The Ghost is the best.'

After the raid, it was said Basil had made off with most of the cash, leaving the other gang members with the jewellery and diamonds, which were harder to dispose of. Consequently, he stayed out of the exchange, which led to the arrest of other gang members.

Perkins and Jones had tried to cheat Basil out of his share, but this seemed to have failed. While they faced long prison sentences, Basil was still at large, probably with much of the loot that had not been recovered.

The *Mirror* said he was a trained engineer who lived less than a mile from Hatton Garden. Single, with no children, he was six foot tall and of slight build. Basil was not thought to be his real name and his greying brown hair was hidden by a ginger wig during the raid. Then in his mid-fifties, he had been involved in a number of burglaries over the past twenty years and had never been caught. Another underworld source has suggested he was a veteran villain 'who always ducks his nut'.

The *Mirror*'s man added: 'He got into crime in his mid-thirties and he didn't need much coaching. Brian recognised his ability and brought him on board.'

The paper even knew that The Ghost's father was dead, although his mother was still alive and his brothers and sisters lived in the UK. The insider believed Perkins's and Jones's attempt to cheat Reader and The Ghost out of their share had led to their downfall. Reader would have made them make the split straight away and they would have disposed of the loot before the police came calling. As it was, The Ghost had not known where to find Perkins or Jones. However, he had known where Collins walked his dog and had tried to find him there.

The newspaper's source said he had spoken to The Ghost soon after the raid and was not sorry that Perkins and Jones had been caught.

'It's poetic justice for those two,' he said, 'but I felt sorry for Brian and The Ghost.'

Since then he had not heard from The Ghost, who he said was probably sunning himself on Spain's Costa del Crime.

In the *Mail on Sunday* veteran crime writer Wensley Clarkson came up with a more intriguing theory. He said that Reader and Perkins must have approached the Adams family for permission for the heist as it was on their patch. The A-Team gave the go-ahead because they wanted to get their hands on the contents of one of the boxes in the Hatton Garden Safe Deposit. The box belonged to John 'Goldfinger' Palmer and contained crucial evidence implicating the A-Team in the murder of a gangland figure. Palmer kept it as insurance, threatening to hand it over to the police if he came to any harm. The feud between the Adams family and Palmer had been going on for thirty years since the Brink's-Mat heist.

Reader and Perkins were also warned not to touch a number of safe deposit boxes belonging to the family. To ensure everything went smoothly, the Adams family wanted their man in on the job: this was Basil. He had access to the building through the family's contacts. His role would be to let them in and disable the alarms, then grab the box that the Adams family wanted. Reader and Perkins were not in a position to say no.

As Basil worked for the Adams family, he was untouchable. None of the crooks that have been captured will say anything about him to the police, even for a reduction in their sentences, even if prosecutors were to review their decision not to pursue the second charge of conspiracy to convert or transfer criminal property, which carries a maximum term of fourteen years and loss of property.

It was agreed that only Basil and Jones were slender enough to get through the hole in the vault wall. Once inside, Basil grabbed the box the family wanted. Then he pocketed the most valuable gems from the vault and there was nothing the rest of the gang could do about it. They could not even grass him up. If Basil was arrested, they would be killed – or worse. In one of his bugged conversations, Jones talked about Tommy Adams 'chopping someone's legs off'.

The gang then feared that Palmer might turn supergrass. It was thought he was co-operating with the police in an attempt to avoid extradition to Spain, where he was wanted for fraud and money laundering. He knew about the heist and could disclose the identity of Basil.

On 24 June 2015, Palmer was found dead at his home in South Weald. Despite his death being initially recorded as 'non-suspicious', the coroner found that he had been shot six times. No one has been charged with the murder.

While Clarkson's theory ties up many of the loose ends, a former barman from a certain pub in Islington told me that he once saw three of his now-infamous regulars disappear into a backroom with someone who has more recently appeared on television as one of the victims of the heist. The mysterious 'Frank the Fence', who handled some of the stolen gems, is also on the run, according to *The Sun*. Clearly, there is more of this story to tell.

Meanwhile, David Pearl gave up plans to turn the vault into a museum. Instead he decided to make it into a restaurant and bar, using the famous hole as a serving hatch. Unfortunately, in the wake of the theft, the hole had been filled in, in an attempt to protect the remaining valuables. So Pearl has had to have the hole re-drilled.

And if there is a movie about the heist, Michael Caine is up for it.

'I read the paper today about the Hatton Garden robbery, and everyone's suggesting that I do the film with Ray Winstone,' he told the press. 'I would do it in an instant.'

That may be some comfort to the old-aged villains eking out their final years in their jail cells. They may find it a fitting commemoration of their audacious crime. After all, in his bugged conversations, Perkins was overheard saying: 'If we get nicked, at least we can hold our heads up that we had a last go, the last fling.'

A last fling indeed. On 9 March 2016, Collins, Jones and Perkins were sentenced to seven years. Wood and Lincoln were given six. Doyle was given twenty-one months suspended for two years and said he intended to appeal the verdict. As of the time of writing, Carl Wood has appealed his sentence.

Reader was handcuffed to a hospital bed after having a second stroke and was too ill to appear. He was to be sentenced later though, given his grave condition, few thought he would last that long.

Perkins said 'Thank you, sir' to the judge before smiling and waving to his family and friends. Jones said 'Thank you judge.' Later, the men could be heard cheering. They would probably be out of jail in three years.

When sentencing them, Judge Christopher Kinch QC paid the Diamond Geezers a backhanded compliment.

'It is clear that the burglary at the heart of this case stands in a class of its own,' he said, 'in the scale of the ambition, the detail of the planning, the level of preparation and the organisation of the team carrying it out, and in terms of the value of the property stolen.'

It seems that the Hatton Garden Heisters had made it into the history books.